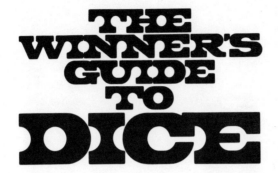

50

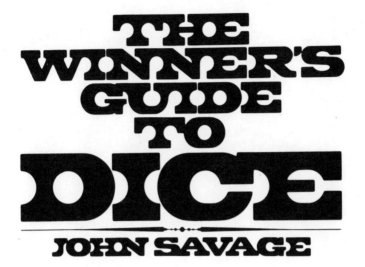

THE WINNER'S GUIDE TO DICE

JOHN SAVAGE

GROSSET & DUNLAP
Publishers • New York

This is for Helen,
who turned pale but did not protest
when I switched to $25 chips

ACKNOWLEDGMENTS

Special thanks are due to Hal Cooper, friend, math wizard, and steady winner, who double-checked the mathematics in this book and confirmed their accuracy.

Bill Johnston, though he doesn't even play craps, gets a low bow for other and very important reasons. But he really ought to try his hand at the game.

J. S.

CONTENTS

INTRODUCTION

There is no faster route to swingers' heaven than to become known at the world's gambling resorts as a man who plays for high stakes.

Thereafter, if you decide you want to spend a weekend, a week or a month in Las Vegas, the Bahamas, Puerto Rico, St. Maarten, Curaçao, Athens, Istanbul or any of the other exotic spots where there are gambling casinos, you can go as an honored guest of the house.

And you go first class—all the way. That includes the flight, accommodations, food, entertainment—everything. If you're unmarried, or married but not a fanatic about it, most of the casinos will even provide you with a plaything of the opposite sex. Hell, the same sex, if you are so inclined.

To a lesser degree, it is the same if you are a

more modest bettor, as long as you are a fairly steady customer. You will probably not be treated quite as royally, but the air fare, hotel room, food and drinks will be on the house.

I don't suppose I am going to knock you over with the announcement that there is a catch to this. The flaw becomes apparent when you end your stay at the resort and find that you are thousands of dollars in the hole, or, worse, that the car, home and business you owned when you arrived have become the property of the casino. Not even the memory of many merry moments in the company of the playthings can make up for it. The trapdoor in heaven has opened, you have fallen through, and you are in hell.

So, the purpose of this book is to instruct, to show you how you can avoid catastrophe, how you can accept all that the house is willing to give and leave the casino as a winner, too. That is, if you restrict your gambling to the crap tables. I can't help you at blackjack or roulette or any of the other games. I find them boring—and, more important, financially less productive—so I don't play them. I am a veteran at craps, however. And what is of more consequence, I am a winner—a **big** winner.

I am not a professional gambler; I am in the publishing business. I will not strain false modesty by claiming, per se, not to be a genius (I may be in my own field, although I wouldn't want to have to prove it). But I will confess to being less than extraordinarily knowledgeable in the fields of mathematics and the occult sciences. I do not use a complicated mathematical formula to win, nor do I consult the stars or carry any part of a dismembered rabbit for good luck.

Put simply, my method consists of knowing what bets to make, when to make them, when to increase the amount of the bets, and when to quit. Some of the information is available to anyone; some of it can be gained only by experience. Here, it is presented in a way that I hope will make it easy for you to understand—and then apply—even if you don't know a crap table from a football rink.

When my wife and I were in our twenties, we spent a vacation in Las Vegas for the first time. The gambling industry there was young then, too. There were none of the skyscraper hotels that there are now, only ranch-style and two-story hotels and motels. We paid our own way and we bet moderately, budgeting ourselves to ten dollars a day—for the two of us, combined.

Today, when we go on one of our frequent gambling vacations, we are as likely to go to London or Istanbul as to Las Vegas, and our expenses are paid by the casino. My average bet is two hundred dollars on each roll of the dice (my wife, less adventurous, is still working with that original ten dollars). And at this point we are so far ahead of the house that we have been playing on their money for years and, as long as we continue to play intelligently, cannot possibly get hurt.

In our last three visits to Las Vegas, for instance, my winnings were $11,000, $20,000 and $19,000 and I have xeroxes of the receipts from the casinos to prove it. If I elected to do so, I could be even further ahead without actually winning any additional money. For there is a way (which I will tell you about) of collecting your winnings without getting the transaction on the record, thereby enabling you to circumvent the income tax collectors. But I tend not to be overly greedy.

And controlling your greed, as you will learn, is a very important factor in becoming a winner at the crap tables.

Now, let's get rolling. . . .

John Savage

●
_____

JUNKETS

To begin with, I am not going to tell you how many craps players there are in the world, how much they lose each year at the game, or how many mouths could be fed or how many bombers could be built (depending on your priorities) if the money were put to a different use. Would you be a better craps player if you knew?

So much for statistics.

The history of the game can be covered about as quickly. Nobody really knows how it got started. It is known, though, that craps was introduced to America by a Frenchman. Today, France is one of the few countries in the world where it is illegal to play craps in a casino. Historical conclusion: Things change, even in France.

The aspect of the game, as it is presently played,

that I find most fascinating is the junket. A junket is when a number of people get together in one place and go somewhere else for a particular purpose. I suppose that is also a description of an army expeditionary force. But let's limit ourselves to gambling junkets, the purpose of which is to gamble.

There are two kinds of gambling junkets, one for so-called VIPs and another for everybody else. Being a VIP, in this instance, does not necessarily mean that you are a Very Important Person in the eyes of society in general. It merely means that you are coveted by the gambling casinos, for the reason that you are a high-stakes bettor and thus are likely to lose a lot of money. Casino owners, not unlike most of us, are somewhat subjective in their judgments of individuals' worth.

There are junkets to all gambling resorts—Las Vegas, Lake Tahoe, Puerto Rico, the Bahamas, Aruba, Greece, Istanbul, and so on. Even Yugoslavia, which thinks of itself as a communist country, has a number of capitalist casinos—the only place in the world where, when you win, you can be said to be "in the Red."

It is possible to go on a junket any week of the year. If one casino isn't running a junket, another is. There are also junkets on holidays—July Fourth, Labor Day, Memorial Day, and so forth. The trips usually extend from Wednesday through Sunday, five days. The planes that take you to the casinos are considerably lighter on the way back because most of the money has been left behind.

One of the major conveniences of traveling to the gambling resorts by junket is that you do not have to carry large amounts of cash. You simply establish credit (called a "credit line") with the junket operator, prior to departure, in the same

Sum Fun:

New "Junket" dates for your Spring/Summer Holiday

...IP INCLUDES: AIR-FARE • HOTEL • FOOD AND BEVERAGES

SCHEDULE

April 25th	to	April 29th
May 2nd	to	May 6th
May 24th	to	May 28th
July 4th	to	July 8th
July 18th	to	July 22nd
August 8th	to	August 12th
August 30th	to	Sept. 3rd

...Vegas

...are cordially invited to the Grand Opening Party
as a Personal Guest of

...ERNATIONAL SPORTSMAN

AT THE NEW AND FABULOUS

...SPANIOLA HOTEL AND CASINO

...TO DOMINGO - DOMINICAN REPUBLIC
THE NEW PLAYGROUND OF THE
AMERICANS
LAND OF FUN AND SUN

MEMORIAL DAY WEEKEND MAY 24 TO 28TH
(HUSBAND AND WIFE ARE OUR GUESTS)

JULY 4TH WEEKEND - JUNE 30TH TO JULY 4...
(HUSBAND AND WIFE ARE OUR GUESTS)

...Maarten Isle

...OTEL & CASINO
...OUR HOSTESS MAY SAMUELS
...RING & HOLIDAY
SPECIALS

The Dunes Hotel & Country Club has chartered United Airlines Jets departing Kennedy Airport on the following Wednesdays:

September 12th — September 26th — October 10th — October 24th

You are invited to be our guest.

As our guest, you will enjoy a luxurious room, superb dining at our many fine restaurants, featuring outstanding cuisine, entertainment and dancing.

This invitation entitles you to transportation, room, food and beverage only. Incidental personal expenses, such as phone calls, tips, laundry, shop purchases, health club, beauty and barber shop service, are not included.

We anticipate many requests for these week-ends. In view of this, please return the enclosed response card promptly.

In order to allow adequate time for check-in, please meet me at the United Airlines Ticket Counter at Kennedy Airport at 12:00 Noon one-and-one-half hours before flight time. The return flight leaves Las Vegas at 5:00 P.M., Las Vegas time, on Sunday.

Please note that this invitation is not transferable.

Sincerely,
John Weintraub
J. "Big John" Weintraub
Al Tolles

Dunes
HOTEL AND COUNTRY CLUB
NEW YORK OFFICE: 16 W. 47th STREET, NEW YORK, N.Y. 10036 / (212) 489-0040

SAHARA
LAS VEGAS, NEVADA

Swing at the Star Studded **Sahara**

MARCH 14 - 18
MARCH 28 - APRIL 1
APRIL 25 - 29
MAY 2 - 6
MAY 24 - 28

BIENVENIDO

CURACAO
NETHERLANDS
ANTILLES

...It's Called

Flamboy...
BEACH HOTEL

Dear VIP: The E San Juan Hotel cordially invites you and your guest to join us Executive Package

THE PROGRAM INCLUDES:
• Air Fare transportation from New York's Kennedy International Airpo...
• Breakfast Luncheon and Dinner (deliciously varied) at restaurants ran... from casual tropical to comfortably luxuriously-elegant
Beverages are of course included (with the exception of fully stocked b... purchases)

PLEASE NOTE THE DATE:

club discoteque gourmet dining nursery

We are arranging for a limited number of VIP Patrons among which y... being invited to spend an exclusive week-end at our 380 acre par...
EL CONQUISTADOR HOTEL & CLUB as a member of our EXEC...
PACKAGE PROGRAM

THE PROGRAM INCLUDES:
Air Fare transportation from New York's Kennedy International Airpo...
San Juan round trip
Ground transportation from San Juan International Airport to El Conquis...
Hotel round trip
Deluxe Air-conditioned Guest Roo...

EVERY WEDNESDAY

including –
DELUXE ROOM ACCOMMODATIONS
ALL FOOD & BEVERAGES
Taxes & Tips (not included)

Travel requirements (proof of citizenship, birth certificate...
...pter's registration...

M. C. TOURS INC.

...
...ITE YOU TO RELAX, TRAVEL and GAMBLE!
"The Tiffany of Hotels"
...wing every Wednesday-Sunday or Sunday-Thursday
...th-12th August 22nd-26th September 26th—
...Most beautiful vacation spot in the West
...N ISLANDS: Weekly trips, Wednesday-Sunday
...: Weekly trips, Wednesday-Sunday, Choice
...Labor Day 6 day trip, August 29th - September
...er 12th - 16th, wives free, please be our que...
...HOTEL, K.R.K. JUGOSLAVIJA on the Adriatic Sea
...1st, August 14th, August 21st, August 28th, S...
...er 11th, September 18th, September 25th
...HOTEL, PULAS, JUGOSLAVIJA on the Adriatic Se...
...Trip leaving weekly
...Special trip...

Dunes
HOTEL AND COUNTRY CLUB
...K OFFICE: 16 W. 47th STREET, NEW YORK, N.Y. 10036 / (212) 489-0040

May Samuels
cordially invites a select number of men, and their wives, to jo...
in a gala vacation to fabulous

CASINO BLE...

Golf Hotel Bled, Yuge...

The Fourth of July Holiday

...ly 3rd to July 8th

...re cordially invited....

americana
OF SAN JUAN

A Very Special Invitation

Jeff Woods is pleased to announce...
...appointment as New York representative...
"Circus Circus Hotel-Spa-Casino...
...Vegas newest luxury hotel and only...

You are cordially invited to be a
Very Special Guest
for a truly outstanding
Las Vegas holiday at Circus Circus...

...suddenly depandeure... We are indeed...

A.S.A.P.
Please contact Jeff Woods
551 Fifth Avenue - Suite 1801
New York, N.Y. 10017
Phone (212) 697-7721

...Office
...Avenue
...rk, New York 10036
Mr. ...

...re-introduce you to the luxurious, oceanfront Americana
...Juan and its action packed casino, we are pleased to invite
...l your wife for a four-day complimentary stay including
...te food and beverage privileges at this most swinging spot
...rto Rico.

...hile at the Americana, you are also invited to be our guests...
...nner and show at our theatre restaurant. Featuring Barry
...'s spectacular "Revue Royale de Paris ", this is one
...ght of your trip you...

Lucaya's even livelier at Lucayan Bea...

Labor Day Special

We have planned a special Mr. and M...
Labor Day Trip
to the Fabulous Lucayan Beach Hote...
Freeport, Grand Bahamas
for a limited group of our friends.
We have chartered two special Delta Jet Air...
Leaving J.F.K. Airport

way that you would establish credit with any other organization. That credit line is then good at the casino.

When you enter the casino to play for the first time and request chips, the pit boss will ask you what your name is, the amount of chips you desire, and what junket you are on (whispering so that the conversation cannot be overheard by any of the Internal Revenue Service agents who are planted in the casinos). After the pit boss has checked your credit, you will receive chips in the amount that you requested. Then the pit boss will have you sign a marker for the amount. After you become known at the casinos, all you will have to do to get chips on credit is ask for them.

When you end up a winner, you call for your markers, pay them with chips, and tear up the markers. You then go to the cashier's window and turn in the rest of your chips for cash. The cash can be kept in a safe-deposit box provided by the hotel. And, if you have accumulated a great deal of cash by the end of your stay, you can exchange it for a "safekeeping" receipt. It is not necessary, incidentally, to buy back your markers every time you leave the table. You can pay them off at the end of the trip, or a few days or a week or two later, after you have returned home.

There are trips to the casinos, too, operated by some airlines and travel agencies. But these are not true junkets; they are simply ways of selling airplane tickets. There are no VIPs, nor plebians, on these trips. Everybody pays and everybody gets the same "package." The only advantage is—and it is minor—that the rate is slightly lower than usual.

Also, there are so-called junkets on which you are expected to put up front money. That is, you pay, say, one thousand dollars in advance and get that amount of credit at the crap tables. Thus you don't have to begin betting from your pocket until after you have lost the thousand dollars.

The object of this latter plan—fairly obviously—is to make sure that you **do** play at the tables. No deadheads are wanted. If it were possible, the casinos would require a loyalty oath from all visitors, requiring them to swear to bet a certain amount at the gambling games. Patriotism would be measured by dollars lost.

But on the real, honest-to-God, genuine junkets, transportation, hotel accommodations, food and drinks are free. The casinos assume that the people who take advantage of this opportunity are responsible adults who will do their duty and lose their money at the gambling games without having to be led by the hand. They pay only their incidental expenses—tips, golfing fees, haircuts and the like—and, of course, their gambling losses.

The difference is in the degree of generosity extended to the VIPs and the plebians. The extra considerations that a VIP receives make what is a bargain in the first place even more attractive. A VIP gets the kind of treatment that is usually lavished on visiting royalty. For instance, when a dice table gets hot and at the same time gets crowded, the dealers will always make room for a VIP. And that is extremely important. A hot table is a winning table. But it isn't any good to you if you can't get to it. The problem is solved when the dealer commands the sea of players around the table to part, making an opening for you to the promised land.

Can you go on a VIP junket and not gamble for high stakes? It happens. But, like the Shadow, the house knows. If you try it a second time, you will be presented with a bill for your transportation, accommodations, etc. And if you refuse to pay, you find out how those gorillas who appear to be standing around the casino doing nothing earn their keep.

The shows at the hotels are big and lavish and, as we used to say back in the days when MGM owned show business, star-studded. The entertainers range from Wayne Newton to Johnny Cash—not a vast distance, but enough to include Petula Clark, Harry Belafonte, Don Ho, Bill Cosby, Bobbie Gentry, Bob Newhart, Tony Bennett, Liberace, Diana Ross and so on.

Naturally, when a name entertainer is appearing, there is always a long line of waiting customers at the entrance to the main room. These lines are things to behold. They wind in and out, stretching for distances that are comparable to city blocks. Judge Crater has been standing in one of the lines since August, 1930, and he still hasn't got in to see Al Jolson.

But a VIP is above standing in lines of any kind. Usually the hotel holds back several reservations for the shows. These reservations are given to VIPs, allowing them to bypass the lengthy lines and walk in and see the show whenever they happen to arrive. This is called having a "walk in" pass.

Even more satisfying to the ego is getting in without having a reservation. If a reservation has not been made, the VIP is requested to "see Joe"— or whatever the name might happen to be—at the casino. Joe will personally escort the VIP past the line. An especially coveted VIP will be taken in through the kitchen and seated at a front table. If no front table is available at the moment, a new front table will be set up in front of the old front tables. Anything can be arranged. There is something of the old gangster movie about it, and I have been tempted, while being personally escorted, to flip a silver dollar, George Raft style.

The accommodations? A VIP does not get a room, a VIP gets a suite. Plus niceties. Rescue parties of waiters are constantly arriving with lifesaving provisions of liquor, fruit and flowers. It is marvelous if you are an alcoholic on a banana and grape diet, but mildly distressing if you are a hay fever sufferer and the hotel has just gotten a good deal on goldenrod.

And then there are the ladies. The invitation to go on a VIP junket is for the VIP and wife—at no extra cost—or "friend." But the VIP who does not have a wife or friend to take along (or, having one or both, chooses to take neither), need not be without female companionship while he is at the hotel. All he has to do is let his desire be known and when he retires to his suite after a night at the crap tables he will find a lady in the bed. The lady will not have blundered into the room by mistake.

I can report on these young ladies' proficiency and enthusiasm for their chosen sport only by hearsay. When I go junketing my wife goes with me, by mutual choice. But the word is that they are multitalented and plentiful.

Regarding the latter, I have a friend who, to test the hotel's affection for him, asked to have a different young lady sent to his suite each night. The hotel honored the request. Still not convinced that the hotel's affection for him was genuine, he asked for a change of ladies **during** the night, one for before he went to sleep, another for when he woke up. The house came through without even a mutter. My friend no longer doubts that he is sincerely loved.

A word of caution about these ladies, however: Don't let your ego persuade you that they are in your bed for any but business reasons. Their business and the casino's business. They are paid for going to bed with you. Their act requires them to give you the impression that you are a great lover. It goes with the atmosphere.

But, face it, even if you are a great lover, the lady could not care less. When you leave, the next "John" will become her great lover. She is doing her job. Her job is to keep you content, so that when you go to the tables to play you will put caution aside and bet casually and foolishly. That is what the casino is paying her for; not to satisfy your sexual need, but to turn you into an idiot at the gambling tables.

TO JUNKET OR NOT TO JUNKET

If you intend to go gambling, how could a junket possibly be a bad deal? With the costs either entirely or mostly taken care of by the house, there seems no way that you could lose—as far as expenses are concerned, that is.

There are those, though, who claim that junkets are snares and should be avoided. The contention is that the party atmosphere on junkets can lead to indiscriminate betting at the casino and thus to big losses.

I agree that the junket is a snare. The hotel's reason for treating you like royalty, obviously, is to get you into the casino, where it is hoped—and the chances are good—that you will lose heavily. The hotels at gambling resorts are not profit makers. They probably don't even break even.

They are there and they are luxurious because if they weren't, fewer players would be at the gambling tables, where the money is made. The hotels and the attractions they provide—the big-name shows, the posh restaurants, and so on—are come-ons for the casinos. Las Vegas is the world's biggest and most brightly lighted billboard.

Part of the lure **is** the party atmosphere. The party begins when you board the plane that will take you to the resort. The booze flows. You're with fellow gamblers and the talk is easy and convivial. Before the plane even takes off, you find, happily, that you are with your kind of folks. Naturally, you want to impress them. What are real friends for, if not to admire you?

The temptation is to continue the party when you get to the crap tables. To continue to show off, to bet big and indiscriminately to prove to your new-found friends that you are so affluent that you can lose big without being hurt by it. It is something like doing your magic trick at a dinner party after you've had a few drinks. Only, in this case, instead of ruining the host's dinner when you try to yank the tablecloth out from under the dishes, you are your own victim.

From that standpoint—if you can't go to the party and keep your head—it would seem wise to avoid junkets. But the fact is that the party does not stop when you get off the plane. It goes on and on. In the casino the mood is predominantly jubilant. Beautiful young women move among the players, passing out free drinks. Most of the players are on holiday and—win or lose—determined to have fun.

So the fault, dear Brutus, is not in accepting all those freebies from the casino, but in ourselves. If you don't keep your head when you go to the crap tables, the only difference made by not taking what the house is offering is that it will cost you more. Not only will you lose at the tables, but you will also have to pay for your own plane ride, hotel room, food and booze.

My rule is: Take the junket and everything the house will give—then rub it in by winning at the tables.

VEGAS—THE STRIP AND DOWNTOWN

If, after reading this book, you decide you want to try your hand at casino craps, you will probably go to Las Vegas because, today, that is where most of the gambling is done. Vegas is the gambling supermarket, while the other resorts, in comparison, are mere neighborhood groceries.

So, to prepare you if you have never visited there, a few words on Las Vegas:

The city's heart is the Strip, the stretch of luxury hotels that house the big-time casinos. The other organs of the body proper—shopping centers, housing developments, outdoor recreational facilities—stand as close to the heart as possible, acutely aware that their existence depends on the flow of money that it pumps into them.

The hotels on the Strip are larger than life. They provide the guests with every luxury and every convenience. The carpeting is thick, the rooms and suites are king-size, the furnishings are elegant, and the service is next to unbelievable. Even if you leave your room for only a few minutes, it seems, a maid darts in to change the towels. It is a tourists' paradise.

That, of course, is the idea behind the Strip. To cater to the tourists, the passers-through, who, over a period of a few days, will drop their bundles, then ease out of town, lighter in the poke but still happy in the heart. Even if you lose, just being there is a dazzling experience.

But, just as midtown Manhattan is not all there is to New York City, the Strip is not the total of Las Vegas. For gamblers, there is also Downtown. Downtown begins where the Strip ends. It is the casino section known as "Glitter Gulch"—for the reason that even during the darkest time of night its bright lights give it the look of high noon. There is always plenty of action Downtown, but, in comparison to the action on the Strip, it is penny ante.

My first experience with Downtown was my last. I went there out of curiosity. What kept me from going again was the discovery that I could have won big at the crap tables and carried off my entire winnings in a coin-changer. The casino I entered was crammed with cab drivers, cowboys, bellhops, past-their-prime showgirls, off-duty bartenders, store clerks and so on, who were playing all of the games that were available on the Strip, plus a few more—faro, bingo, keno. By chance, I found a hot dice table almost immediately. And disillusionment came as quickly.

When I bought chips, I found that they were not worth five dollars and twenty-five dollars, as the colors indicated to me, but nickels and quarters. An hour or so of playing produced a profit of a little over twenty-five dollars. The same time spent at a Strip casino would have given me winnings of a hundred times that much.

So, if you go to Las Vegas to win big, stay away from Downtown. The profit rate is too low. You can do as well or better on the Strip in a fraction of the time. It is one of the instances when time really is money.

SOME PLAIN TRUTHS

There is no possible way that you can make a full-time job of playing craps—eight hours a night, five nights a week—and win. That seems like a contradiction of the title of this book, I realize. But it isn't. The key word is: full-time. You **can** win. But not if you play the game day in and day out as regularly as you work at your job or profession.

There is no magic formula. If there were, there would be no crap tables at the casinos. The players with the magic formula would long ago have made craps unprofitable for the casino owners. And the owners have crap tables in the casinos for one reason: to make money for them.

What you can do is win occasionally. You can do this by playing intelligently—by knowing what factors control the game and playing only when those factors are most in your favor. This requires not playing when the factors are against you, which is why you can't work full-time at playing craps. Most of the time the factors that control the game are not in your favor.

There are professional gamblers, of course, who do quite well financially. But most of the people who are thought of as professional gamblers are not really gamblers at all. They are businessmen; gambling is their business. They book bets—it is the people who place the bets with them who are doing the gambling. The so-called professional gamblers will not book a bet unless the factors that control it are in their favor.

The same applies to the casinos. When you play craps at a casino, the house is booking your bet. You are betting that when the dice are rolled a certain result will occur. The house covers that bet, but it covers it in such a way that you, the bettor, have a considerably greater chance of losing than winning.

Just as there would be no crap tables in the casinos if there were a magic formula for winning, there would also be no crap tables if no player ever won. Not even the fanatics would play if there were no chance at all of winning. So, that is what this book is about: the times when a player **can** win, if he follows certain rules.

MOST PLAYERS LOSE

The jokes around the casinos are predominantly of the black-humor school. There is the story about the big loser who arrived in Las Vegas in a $9,000 Cadillac but saw a ray of sunshine in the fact that he departed on a $60,000 bus. Another story has it that one habitual loser was finally visited by a stroke of exceptional luck—he was killed in an automobile accident on his way from the airport to the casino.

There is a good reason why most of these jokes are told at the expense of the bettors. It is telling it like it is, sardonic recognition of the fact that most bettors do lose. There are glowing tales, too, about big winners. But those stories are few. And nobody seems to know where the big winners are at present. Most of them exist in memory only. The fact of the matter is probably that after making a killing the big winners went back to the tables and quickly rejoined the big losers.

That happened to a pair of friends of mine a few years ago. I'll call them Paul and Mary. Like my wife and me, they occasionally took vacations to gambling resorts. They both played craps, usually losing, but never disastrously.

Mary decided that it would be pleasant to be a winner—something to tell the "girls" at bridge. She induced Paul to join in a pact. On their next trip, when they were ahead at the crap tables, they would quit—cold—and send the winnings home, as I had advised them to do, thereby making certain that they would not lose the money back to the casino.

In due time they arrived in Las Vegas. The first night Paul got lucky and won over $30,000. He and his wife were ecstatic. Mary reminded Paul of the pact. Paul resisted. He had a feeling that he was on an unbeatable streak, a premonition that he could win even bigger. If he stayed at the table, he could turn the thirty thousand into sixty thousand, maybe even a hundred thousand.

Mary insisted that the pact be kept. Paul con-

tinued to argue. They left the casino and went to
their suite, still debating, Mary standing firm and
Paul pleading for flexibility. He pointed out that
he'd had "feelings" before and that they'd always
proved valid. Hadn't he had a premonition of doom
just before their son had fallen out of a tree house
and broken his arm? Hadn't he had a feeling that
something good was going to happen just before
they received notice that Uncle Arnold had died
and left them the beach property?

But Mary was deaf to all reason. Finally Paul
gave in, dismal in defeat. He handed Mary the
money and told her to get a check for it from the
casino, and then mail it back home. As for him,
he was exhausted; he was going to bed.

Mary left the suite with the money. Paul retired
and immediately dropped off to sleep. But he woke
a few hours later, disturbed by a subconscious
premonition that something was wrong. Mary was
not in the suite. He dressed quickly, intending to
go looking for her. But as he was about to depart,
she returned—looking sheepish.

Where had she been? She had been to the casino. What had she been doing in the casino? Well,
on the way to exchange the cash for a check, she
had thought about all that Paul had been saying.
It was true, she admitted to herself, that his pre-
monitions usually proved out. Suppose he was
right this time, too? Suppose he really was on an
unbeatable streak? Was it fair for her to deny him
the opportunity to win $100,000?

To test the possibility that her husband's luck
was indestructible, Mary went to the crap tables
and made a small bet. She won. Still skeptical, she
made a larger bet, and won again. Convinced now
that Paul was right, that he was on a streak,

she made a much larger bet—and lost. She felt ashamed. She had violated the pact. She had to make back the money she'd lost. In the process of trying to get even, she lost the entire $30,000.

Naturally, Paul hit the ceiling. Not because she had lost the $30,000, though. Because she had commandeered his lucky streak as her own and in the process of using it had mangled it beyond repair—the same way, years earlier, she had gummed up his electric shaver. He was convinced that the streak would never work for him again. About that, he was thirty thousand percent right.

Since the only logical reason for playing craps is to win and logic tells you that you can't win, why play? The answer is, of course, that losers are not using logic. That doesn't exactly put losing craps players in a league by themselves. In general, a great many things that people do are not based on logic. What is logical, for example, about fashions in clothes? But skirt lengths continue to rise and fall. And would anybody be surprised if spats came back into fashion next year?

Not all craps players reject logic to the same degree. There are those for whom beating the house is a compulsion. They lose everything of value—mates, children, jobs, property—trying to become big winners at the crap tables, or, having lost their initial stake, attempting to get even.

Psychologists say that the compulsive bettor knows what he is up against and doesn't really want to win, that he wants to lose in order to punish himself. If that is the case, these masochists have certainly found a surefire way of giving themselves a symbolic thrashing; the only thing a bettor has to do to guarantee that he will get beaten is to stand at the crap tables long enough. A shellacking is inevitable.

So if your aim is to beat the bank at Las Vegas, this book is not for you. Your dream is infantile. Instead of reading on, I suggest that you (1) write up your compulsion in the form of a scenario and get yourself a good agent—things like that **do** happen in the movies, or (2) consult a psychiatrist; maybe a doctor can help you find out what it is that a casino represents to you that makes you want to "beat" it, and then, failing that, "get even," or (3) join Gamblers Anonymous.

In between the compulsive bettors and the bettors who win are the players for whom betting at craps is an adventure. They win sometimes—just often enough to whet the appetite—and lose a great deal more often. Primarily they are at the casino for the fun of it, but secretly they harbor the conviction that they can win consistently—if only they get lucky.

If these in-between bettors don't win, they don't feel that the world has ended; they simply go back to where they came from and pick up their lives where they left off, manufacturing ball bearings or publishing books or rooting out sewers with their rotors, happy to have had a jolly holiday. Next time, however, it will be different, they tell themselves: not only will they have a jolly holiday, but they will also win at craps—if only they get lucky.

These are the players the casinos love. They lose cheerfully. And, because they believe that with a little luck they can eventually win, they return to the casinos every chance they get and lose cheerfully over and over again. They are the true suckers—as opposed to the compulsive bettors, who are merely sick. Las Vegas is their monument. Where there was desert, they planted their dollars, and the neon bloomed, lighting up the sky all the way to Brooklyn.

EXCITEMENT

I can understand how those bettors can go home lighter in the bankroll but happy. Playing craps in a casino can be exciting and satisfying even if you lose. The crap table is where the action is. And that is what most players are at the casino for—to escape from the everyday routine, to have a fling, to live it up.

When you enter the gaming room at a casino you will invariably find that the majority of the players are at the crap tables. There are customers, too, of course, at the roulette wheels, the blackjack tables, the wheel of fortune, the slot machines and other games, but it is always the crap tables that are crowded.

I think that is because craps provides the players with a kind of gratification not offered by other games. For one thing, there is personal involvement. When you are the shooter you hold the dice in your hand and roll them, creating the illusion that you have a hand, so to speak, in what is going to happen, that with your throw you can influence the outcome.

There is no such feeling when you are playing the other games. You are not really participating, you are observing; you aren't running with the ball, you are sitting in the stands. You don't personally spin the roulette wheel or the wheel of fortune. In blackjack the deck is in the hands of the dealer. And playing a slot machine is about as impersonal as corresponding by form letter with IBM.

But even if you are not shooting (some players never take the dice), you feel personally involved because of the variety of bets available: you can bet with the dice or against the dice; you can bet on particular numbers; by betting certain ways, you can alter the odds against you. This variety gives you the opportunity to use your mind, to outwit "luck," whereas, in most of the other games, you are subject entirely to the vagaries of chance.

Another factor which makes craps so popular is that it offers you the opportunity to win big—and quickly. When the dice get hot it is possible to run a small stake into a big win very fast. Most craps players have seen this happen and are very conscious of it. What they forget—block out, that is—is that it is far easier to run a large stake into a big loss even faster.

But the losses also contribute to the excitement. The players are aware that a duel is in progress—themselves against the house. The knowledge that more often than not the players will lose does not in the least dull the anticipation. On the contrary, it makes winning even more desirable. Isn't it more of a feat to win against big odds than against small odds? They know it is possible to win. They see it happening. And, ever optimistic, they assume that they can do it too—if only they get a little lucky.

This anticipation—the expectation that the next roll of the dice will produce a winning number—results in a great deal of verbalizing at the crap tables. The bettors encourage the shooter—the player who is about to roll the dice—and each other. And the shooter talks to the dice, exhorting them to perform in a winning way. When the dice oblige, there are, naturally, shouts of exultation. And when the dice prove stubborn, of course, cries of agony are heard.

But whether the vocalizing is joyous or mournful, the point is: there is noise. There is hubbub. One roll of the dice is quickly followed by another roll. Something is always happening. A loss is rapidly followed by another opportunity to win. There is no time for prolonged grief. Eldorado is always just over the next rise—and the next rise is only seconds away. Wheeeeeee! Craps is the roller coaster!

LUCK

It is no wonder that the suckers go home happy. They have been taken for a ride, but it's been a thrilling ride, with the chance of winning coming every few minutes. And every once in a while the possible has actually happened—the dice have come up right and won their bets. And, as they all know, with a little more luck, they could have won more often than they lost.

I have yet to be told by a businessman or executive that he became successful because he was lucky. Success in business or at an occupation, to hear them tell it, is always a consequence of astuteness. Yet at craps they look to luck to make them winners.

What they either do not realize or refuse to accept—possibly because it might take some of the fun out of it—is that craps is part of the casino owner's business. It's not a game to the house. What the appliance department is to Macy's, the crap tables are to the casino: one of several income-producing operations. It is run in a business-like way, the object being to produce a profit.

So, the intelligent way to look at craps is as a business operation. When the player steps up to the crap table he should have in mind the fact that he is entering into a business competition with the house, not a battle of wills with the dice. And he should respond to the challenge with astuteness, not with the idea that winning or losing depends on luck or the lack of it.

But, illogically, luck is what most craps players hope for. And, what is even more baffling is that a great many of them compound the initial error by relying on superstitions and/or systems to bring them that luck. It's a little like going to Macy's appliance department and expecting to get a refrigerator at less than wholesale because you have a rabbit's foot in your pocket. Business doesn't work that way.

SUPERSTITIONS AND SYSTEMS

Superstitions are exercises in implausibility. One man I know once had a winning night at the crap tables and discovered when he returned to his hotel suite that at some time during the evening a penny had dropped into his left shoe. When he plays craps now, he always carries a penny in his left shoe. What possible effect could a penny in a shoe have upon the way the dice come up?

The man admits that there is no known method by which the penny in his shoe could influence the dice. He even admits, confidentially, that in spite of the presence of the penny he continues to be a loser. Yet he would not think of going to the crap tables without Abraham Lincoln riding between his sock and his insole—"for luck." I suspect that he believes he would be an even bigger loser if it weren't for the luck the penny brings him.

There are even more ridiculous superstitions. Another acquaintance of mine circles the casino in a cab exactly thirteen times before he enters to play. He explains that he is "standing up" to the number thirteen—if that is an explanation. His theory is that he is defying the supposedly unlucky number, confronting it eyeball to eyeball, and facing it down, thereby sending ill fortune packing. But he's still a loser. The number thirteen evidently sneaks back into town as soon as he enters the casino.

One of the saddest human dramas I know occurred when a man mixed superstition with craps. He was a top executive in a large corporation, and at least once a month he took a few days off and went to Las Vegas to relax at craps. He always lost. But he didn't mind too much. For one reason, he could afford to lose. But, more importantly, he always took a "secretary" with him. These secretaries were invariably beautiful, with a facility for feigning passion.

Once, however, when he attended a business convention in Las Vegas and a secretary did not seem particularly appropriate to the occasion, he took his wife with him. On that trip, as it happened, he had phenomenal luck at the crap tables, winning close to $20,000.

Was he pleased? Not exactly. The implication was much too clear. When he had a beautiful and talented secretary with him, he lost. When he was accompanied by his plain and sexually orthodox wife, he won.

The executive experimented. The next month he took another secretary with him to Las Vegas—and lost. A month later he took his wife with him once more—and won. There was no more doubt about it in his mind; when it came to winning or losing at craps his companion made the difference. Suddenly it became important to him to win. He was an aggressive, goal-directed man, and in his less-than-lucid moments he began dreaming the compulsive gambler's dream of "breaking the bank."

The dilemma, of course, was: to enjoy himself in Las Vegas and lose, or to have a miserable time and win. He chose the latter of the alternatives. Nowadays when he takes his monthly trips to Las Vegas his wife goes along. He has never won again. And the brief periods when he is not at the crap tables are sheer hell, because the extent of his wife's "talent" is a natural immunity to sea-sickness when afloat on a water bed. But he still keeps going back, and taking his wife with him, convinced that in time he will become a big winner.

Superstition, in short, is a blind conviction that reality can be consistently overcome if the faith is strong enough. Logic **has** been bested, true, but the instances are phenomena. And no amount of unreasoning faith has ever converted a phenomenon into a regularly occurring event.

In my own business, for example, if a novel with a seagull as a hero were to become a runaway bestseller, it would be a phenomenon, defying most of the rules of publishing logic. Assuming that the publisher of such a book was wearing his socks on his ears the day he sent it out into the cruel world to compete for the book buyers' dollars, it is not even remotely possible for him to do the same with another book simply by wearing his socks on his ears again. If it were that easy, every book would be a bestseller, and no publisher's ears would ever see the light of day again.

Now, having denounced superstitions, I am going to seem to be contradicting myself by advising you to heed certain signs that, on the surface, appear to have at least a tenuous link with the occult. What I am going to say, in fact, may make me sound as much like a nut as my friend who carries a penny in his shoe. But the difference is that I have seen these things happen in instance after instance, while the penny has yet to change my friend's luck.

For instance, when a shooter is hot, rolling winning number after winning number, and the dice fall to the floor, the experienced player will temporarily withdraw from the game. For he knows that, more often than not, when the game resumes, the roll will be ice cold.

If that doesn't have the character of a superstition, what does? But it isn't. It is something that, over the years, I—and other experienced players—have seen occur too often to discard as an irrelevant quirk. And when it does happen, we pull back.

I can't explain it with mathematics, but I do have a theory. I think the distraction causes the shooter to lose the rhythm that he has developed and which has been the basis for the hot roll. Crazy? Then, in baseball, why does a hot hitter suddenly go into a slump? Most often it is because, temporarily, he has lost his "swing"—his rhythm. If it can happen to hitters, why not to craps shooters?

That explanation, of course, evokes two more

questions. **Do** shooters have a rhythm, and, if so, can that rhythm affect the behavior of the dice?

To answer the first question: all people have a rhythm. Everybody handles himself differently when he moves. After a while, each individual's style becomes recognizable. We can usually recognize someone close to us from a great distance by his or her walk, for instance. The walk is one of the more obvious manifestations of the person's rhythm.

Can that rhythm affect the roll of the dice? There are players who have uncommon luck as shooters (although not necessarily as bettors). Frequently—though, of course, not always—they will roll number after number, avoiding sevening out. Regulars at the dice tables know them and are always delighted to see them take the dice, hopeful that a hot roll is coming.

I can't believe that luck plays any part in the process (if they are so lucky, why doesn't the luck also extend to betting?). I am convinced that it is their rhythm—their swing—that produces numbers instead of sevens. How? That I can't explain. But I can't explain how one baseball player's rhythm makes him a better hitter than most of his teammates, either.

Just as dice are the same, baseball bats are essentially the same. A heavier bat can't make a poor hitter into a good hitter. If it could, there would be no poor hitters. They would simply switch to heavier bats and become good hitters. It is the swing—the rhythm—that makes the difference, with shooters as with hitters.

I have also often seen a player or group of players root a table hot with unbridled enthusiasm, by exhorting, cajoling and commanding the dice to perform winningly and spectacularly. I have a sort of theory about how that happens, too. I'm not entirely serious about it, but at least it's a semi-tongue-in-cheek explanation for something I have seen happen with startling regularity. Perhaps it is a demonstration of what scientists call telekinesis: the ability to move inanimate objects by "mind power," without touching the objects; the power that mediums claim to use to raise a table off the floor without touching it.

Scientists tell us that we use only five percent of our brain. I don't believe in mediums or their claims, but isn't it possible that somewhere within the other ninety-five percent of our brains we have a power that, under certain conditions, we use without knowing it? If that power exists, perhaps the players who are rooting a table hot are using it, focusing it on the dice, manipulating them with it.

Anyway, I have seen both things happen often enough to be impressed. When the dice drop to the floor, I call off my bets for the next two rolls. And when I see a group of players going all out to warm up a pair of dice, I stick around to see what will happen, and more often than not I am glad I did— because the dice get hot.

SYSTEMS

I do not give that much credence to systems, though. If believing in superstitions is a blindness of the mind, then following systems is a mental astigmatism. I give systems a little more credibility than superstitions because most systems are based on mathematics. Loosely based, however. And a formula is not necessarily valid merely because it uses numbers. Computers function by means of mathematics, too, but it is common knowledge that what comes out of a computer depends entirely on what goes into it.

I won't try to describe all of the various systems in detail because that would be giving them too much credibility, and also because there are too many of them—as many as there are losers at craps. In general, though, there are two kinds of systems: those that call for betting in multiples and those that depend on the dice coming up in certain patterns.

When you bet in multiples, you double your bet each time you lose, hoping to get back on the next bet what you lost on the preceding one. For instance, a bettor begins with a ten-dollar bet, loses, makes a twenty-dollar bet on the next roll, loses, makes a forty-dollar bet on the next roll, loses, makes an eighty-dollar bet on the next roll, and so on.

Theoretically, that would work. When you finally won a bet, you would get back your losses. But the house protects itself against that by setting a betting limit. Say the limit—the most that can be wagered on any one bet—is five hundred dollars. Betting in multiples, the bettor quickly reaches that limit. Doubling a ten-dollar bet, for instance, a bettor would be betting $320 on the sixth roll and could not double it because the figure would be over the limit. So, clearly, betting in multiples works only if the winning roll comes up quickly, and there is no guarantee that that will happen.

Betting patterns has a little more going for it. The dice do fall in patterns. But those patterns emerge only over a long period of time, and within those periods there is great variation. Consequently, expecting the patterns to prove out over a period of time is tantamount to depending on pure chance.

A pattern bettor will stand at the table, not playing, observing a particular number. Say the number is twelve. When he has determined that the number twelve has not come up in, say, sixty rolls, he will assume—based on the pattern he is following—that it **will** come up within the next thirty rolls. He will then give the dealer thirty chips, requesting that the number twelve be bet for him on the next thirty rolls (one chip, of whatever denomination, on each roll).

For the pattern system to work, though, the patterns would have to be exact over a short period of time and would have to repeat in that same way time after time. The dice are just not that dependable. Within the long period of time there is no "sense" at all to the way they perform. They are as unpredictable as runaway balloons.

The ultimate in contradiction is the player who relies on both a system **and** a superstition. A system is supposedly based on logic—mathematics—while a superstition employs faith to overcome logic. This breed of player—and they are about as numerous and hyperactive as gnats at an outdoor butchering—expects both logic and illogic to work for him at the same time.

Systems are moderately profitable, but only for the hangers-on who sell them to the suckers. A couple of obvious questions arise: If the systems work at the tables, why aren't the devisers of the systems at the tables, cleaning up? Why, instead, are they peddling their valuable systems to other players?

ARE THE DICE LOADED?

It is claimed by most law enforcement agencies that the gambling casinos, especially in Las Vegas, are controlled by the underworld. I don't know for a fact that that is true, but I have no reason to doubt it, and my observations tell me that it probably is true.

If the casinos are owned by gangsters, doesn't it follow, then, that the games are crooked? I am completely convinced that the answer is no. Not because I think the casino owners would hesitate for even a split instant to cheat if it were to their advantage, but because I believe that, on the contrary, their advantage lies in keeping the games honest.

In Las Vegas, an initial investment of as much as twenty million dollars is required to open a hotel-casino. That is enough to make the owners nervous; at times, almost psychotically so. In the back of their minds is the fear that Las Vegas, as a gambling spa, will suddenly lose its popularity. Take the gambling away from Las Vegas and what do you have left? The world's most overcapitalized and underpopulated oasis.

The owners, consequently, are acutely aware of how fickle the public fealty can be. Not every toy endures like the yo-yo. And, though the fear is probably not realistic, they live with the dread that some other spa will suddenly supplant Las Vegas as the gambling capital of the world in the same way that years ago the skateboard supplanted the hula-hoop. See? Build your castle on sand and you become a sure prospect for ulcers.

As a result, the underworld is especially hard

on criminals in Las Vegas. They support their local police with a zeal that even the Birch Society would find impressive. That is because the Las Vegas law enforcement organization concentrates on keeping out freelance thieves and cheats. The object, of course, is to give visitors to the town the feeling that they are safe—on the streets, in their hotel rooms and in the casinos.

To promote further this notion of safety, an attempt was made at one time to bribe the most prominent Las Vegas publisher to keep stories of local crime out of his newspaper. The bribe was rejected. When a crime occurs and it is "booked" by the police, it is reported. But, with the police— in fact, all Las Vegans—so sympathetic to the casino owners' desire to keep the city at least looking clean—and, thus, to keeping the tourists coming—we will probably never know how many crimes go unbooked.

Inside the casinos, the owners have their own security forces. These security men are deputized by the sheriff. They usually mingle with the customers, but, being seven feet tall—all of them—they are about as inconspicuous as basketball centers at a pygmy convention.

If you should happen to see a security man escort a customer from the casino, don't bother to ask what the trouble was. In response you will get a perplexed expression and a reply something like, "What trouble?" Nothing untoward ever occurs at the casinos; even if you see it happen, it is a figment of your imagination.

My conviction that the casinos do not cheat is not based on the loyalty of the local police nor the presence of the security men, but on the fact that the casinos do not have to cheat. The odds (which we will discuss in detail in another chapter) are in the casino's favor. And the majority of players do not play intelligently. Either because they do not make the effort to learn how to win or because, for some psychological reason, they actually want to lose, they seem to bend over backward to make sure that the house ends up with the long, clean end of the stick.

Even when a winning way is well known, most players will not use it if it requires effort. There is an example of that: Several years ago a book on winning at blackjack was published and became a big seller. Basically, the method depends on remembering what cards have been dealt from the top half of the deck and then, by the process of elimination, determining what cards will come from the bottom half of the deck. The method works—for those who have the mind for it and will work at developing it. Players were buying the book, using the method, and winning at the casinos' blackjack tables.

The casinos panicked. They brought in a "shoe," a boxlike apparatus that holds several decks of cards at the same time, and began using four decks at once at the blackjack tables, mixing the cards. The theory was that no one would be able to commit to memory half of that number—two full decks.

The danger passed. Now, because four decks at once are too cumbersome to handle, many of the casinos have reverted to using a single deck, at least on some of their tables. There are still black-jack players who use the method and win. But there are so few of them that they are looked upon by the casinos as merely a minor annoyance. The owners have learned that the vast majority of players will not use a method that requires effort. They remain loyal to the old standby, luck.

The major reason for the casinos' honesty, however, is that dishonesty would eventually drive them out of business. To attract losers it is necessary to have winners. The consistent losers flock to the casinos because they think it is possible for them to win. They have seen others win. They are terminally confident that they can win too. But when they begin to play they discard the logic. Instead of playing the way the winners do, they fall back on superstitions, systems or plain luck.

So, the house likes winners. The house even pampers winners. I am a winner and when I go to the casinos I am treated with loving care. I do not delude myself that I get this preferential treatment because I am such an irresistibly likable fellow (likable, yes; irresistibly, no).

It is because I am a marvelous advertisement for the casinos. And, too, I suspect, because the casino owners have an abiding faith in human nature and are certain that in time I will learn to play as idiotically as most players and lose back to them all that I have won.

But in the meantime I am good for them. I win, I win big, and I make a noise about winning. Everyone at the table—and at most of the other tables—knows that I am making the impossible dream come true: I am beating the house.

For me, this can sometimes be a burden. On a recent trip to Las Vegas, for instance, I was stopped in the lobby of the hotel by a middle-aged man who was a complete stranger to me. The following conversation took place:

He: I want to give you my room number.

Me (mildly taken aback): You must have me mixed up with someone else. I'm a straight.

He: No, you don't get the idea. I been noticing every time there's a hot table, there you are. You turn up like clockwork. My wife keeps saying to me, "There he is again." The idea is: could you do this for me? The next time you see a table getting hot, I'll give you my room number and could you call me?

Instead, I told him how to find a hot table himself. He seemed pleased to have the information, but I doubt that he ever used it. Tracking down a hot table requires effort and time, and he was looking for the magic formula.

The same applies to most of the bettors who are at the table with me when I am winning big. They assume that if I can do it, they can do it. And, in fact, they are right—they **can** do it. The house, however, has no fear that my winning will prove contagious. It knows that there is little chance the other players will suddenly change their ways and cast off their faith in luck, superstitions and systems.

When I think about it, I realize that the casinos ought to be paying me to take their money from them. They don't. So I suppose that makes me an unpaid shill, in a sense. I try not to feel guilty about it, though. I think of myself as spearheading a one-man movement to eradicate gambling by making it unprofitable for the casinos.

Another factor that works against cheating by the casinos is that there are no new ways to do it. Cook up a scheme to rig any gambling game and a little research will show you that it was first conceived by some enterprising Roman back in Caesar's day. Adam, gamblers claim, got Eve's fig leaf in a game of strip poker, using marked cards.

The professionals know all the tricks. If a casino tried to use one, the pros would quickly spot it. Manipulation is impossible to cover up for very long. The professionals detect it and spread the word. If a casino rigged a game, the news would pass from the pros to the public faster than a stack of chips through a hunch bettor's fingers.

Cheating at the crap tables **is** attempted every once in a while, but by players, not by the house. Someone will get possession of a pair of house dice, alter them, then try to slip them into the game. The most common method of altering dice is to shave them—that is, to cut down one side so that the dimensions are changed and the balance is upset. Shaving dice can cause them to turn up sevens (the key number in craps) either more often or less often than the odds dictate, whichever is desired.

The usual way of using altered dice is for two players to work together. One, shooting, will throw the dice hard enough to cause them to fall from the table. His confederate will pick them up and make the switch, palming the game dice and tossing the altered dice onto the table.

But when the dice fall to the floor, a casino employee, usually the boxman, will always examine them thoroughly before putting them back into play. Even if the shooter calls out "same dice," meaning that he wants the fallen dice to continue in play (the shooter, incidentally, is the only player who can request this), the house, of course, will not allow a pair of altered dice to stay in the game.

Players who attempt to cheat are dealt with severely if they try it more than once. The first time they will probably only be taken to the door and warned not to come back. But if they ignore the warning and return and attempt to cheat again, they are handled roughly. In Las Vegas, persistent cheaters are eventually found dead in the desert.

That is not to suggest, though, that you are in danger of being manhandled or rubbed out if you buck heads with the house. Far from it. The casinos, remember, go out of their way to avoid even the appearance of trouble. Casinos are in business. It is to their benefit for the customers to be relaxed and have fun, fun, fun. A player who is having a whopping good time is a player who bets wildly— and loses. A player who enjoys himself is a player who comes back time after time, eager to make the same mistakes all over again.

Consequently, the casinos' motto is: The customer is always right. When there is honest disagreement between the casino and the player, the player is given the benefit of the doubt. For instance, occasionally a bet will get swept from its place. If the bet wins, all the player has to do to get paid off is point out to the dealer what happened. There is no bickering, no looks of disbelief. It is assumed by the house that the player is truthful. Of course, there is a limit to good nature, even if it is in the interests of business. If it becomes obvious that a player is taking advantage of the house's motto, that player is politely escorted to the exit and asked not to come back.

Anyway, I am convinced that the house does not cheat at all and that any cheating done by players does not last long enough to have any appreciable affect on the other players. It is not the dishonest casino nor the slippery player that most bettors have to be wary of—it is themselves. By playing craps as if the outcome depended on sheer luck, the occult or a system, the bettor does more to empty his own pockets than the casino could do if it held a gun to his head.

THE GAME

Now, at last, let's play the game.

In this chapter, I'll discuss the equipment used and the mechanics of making bets. In the next chapter, I'll talk about odds and percentages and some of the subtleties, such as taking and giving odds and buying numbers. After that, I'll be specific about what I think are good bets and bad bets —and why.

First, the equipment.

Casino craps is played on a rectangular table that measures from ten to twelve feet long and three to four feet deep. The surface of the table is covered with green felt. It is bordered by a wooden ledge that has a groove, called a rack, for holding chips.

A DICE TABLE LAYOUT

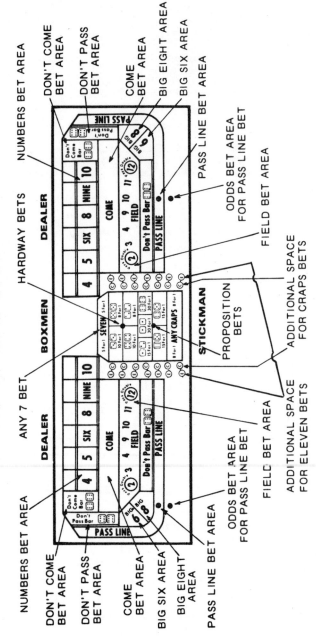

NUMBERS BET AREA

ANY 7 BET

HARDWAY BETS

DON'T COME BET AREA

DON'T PASS BET AREA

NUMBERS BET AREA

COME BET AREA

BIG EIGHT AREA

BIG SIX AREA

PASS LINE BET AREA

ODDS BET AREA FOR PASS LINE BET

FIELD BET AREA

PROPOSITION BETS

ADDITIONAL SPACE FOR CRAPS BETS

ADDITIONAL SPACE FOR ELEVEN BETS

FIELD BET AREA

ODDS BET AREA FOR PASS LINE BET

PASS LINE BET AREA

BIG EIGHT AREA

BIG SIX AREA

COME BET AREA

DON'T PASS BET AREA

DON'T COME BET AREA

NUMBERS BET AREA

Imprinted on the table is a diagram that is referred to as the "layout." To the first-time player the layout usually looks baffling, like one of those puzzles that employs different shapes to test eye-hand coordination. As soon as the uses of the various shapes or sections are understood, however, the puzzlement quickly passes.

The purpose of the diagram is to let the player know what bets are available to him and to give him a place to put his chips when he makes a bet. The two "wings" of the layout are identical, one for the convenience of the players at the right side of the table, the other for the players at the left. In the center is a square, used by both left-side and right-side players.

The wings provide space for making **pass** line bets, **don't pass** line bets, **come** bets, **don't come** bets, **Big 6 And Big 8** bets, **place** bets and **field** bets. In the square, the player makes bets called **hardways, any seven, any crap** and **proposition** bets.

The men who run the table for the casino probably should be listed under equipment too, because—as you will begin to notice after you have played at several casinos—they seem to be as uniform in proficiency as the layouts are in design. Be that as it may, there are at the very least four of these housemen: two dealers, a boxman and a stickman.

The two dealers stand behind the table, one at each side. They pay the winning bets and collect the losing bets. They also place bets for the players who cannot reach a particular section of the layout.

Stationed in a cut-out section of the table, a sort of slot, between the two dealers, is the boxman. He is in charge of the game. He watches the action, handles cash, and has the authority to raise the house limit for a player—the limit being the maximum amount a player can wager on any one bet.

Of the house employees at the table, boxmen are the most interesting to observe. They oversee hundreds of bets and do it with the detached manner of a rock drummer at a violin recital, looking as if they are about to drop off to sleep. But a deviation at the table rarely gets past them. They react as if they are wired to the bets, and irregularities give them an immediate electrical shock. If they could be domesticated, they would make fine home burglar alarms.

And there is the stickman. He stands at the front of the table, between the players at the left and the players at the right and across from the boxman. The stickman is equipped with a long stick with a curved end. He uses it to push the dice to the player who is going to shoot. He also calls the game and handles the various bets in the square.

In a casino, the several crap tables are arranged in more or less of a circle—as if an Indian attack were expected. Inside the circle, a number of additional casino employees wander about, acting mainly as lookouts. They are pitmen—usually senior employees—and are also called pit bosses. The pit boss has the authority to extend, or deny, credit to players. When a table gets hot and the betting is fast and furious, the pitmen move in to assist the boxman in overseeing the action.

Near the stickman is a collection of dice. These are six-sided plastic cubes, each one a little larger than a lump of sugar. A single cube is called a die; two cubes together are referred to as a pair of dice. Each die has six sets of dots (one set on each side) representing the numbers one through six. To be even more specific, the die has a side with one dot, a side with two dots, a side with three dots, a side with four dots, a side with five dots and a side with six dots.

The final item of equipment is the chip. A chip is round and flat, approximately the size of a half-dollar, and made of plastic. Chips are stand-ins for money. They are purchased from the house with money and can be turned back to the house for money. Most commonly, the chips at casinos represent one dollar, five dollars, twenty-five dollars and one hundred dollars.

That's the equipment. Now let's get the game started.

The players stand at the front and sides of the table. They all, in turn, have an opportunity to roll the dice. The player who rolls is called the "shooter." After a player has finished his turn at rolling the dice, they are then given to the player at his left. It is not mandatory for a player to roll the dice, however. If he chooses not to do so, the dice move along to the next player.

The bets are made prior to the roll of the dice (not all kinds of bets can be made on the first roll, but we'll discuss that later). A player makes a bet by placing chips on one or more of the different sections of the layout (**pass** line, **don't pass** line, etc.). The shooter must at the very least make a **pass** or **don't pass** line bet. Not all of the bets that are made will be settled on one roll of the dice, but I'll cover the variations later on. When a bet is finally won or lost, though, the player is either paid his winnings or his chips are immediately removed from the table by the dealer or stickman.

The action begins when the shooter rolls the dice. He throws the cubes out onto the table. Theoretically he must throw them hard enough so that they will hit the backboard (the raised ledge around the table) and rebound. Most casinos, though, are not too particular about that aspect of the roll. The rule about hitting the backboard varies from lax in Las Vegas to firm in Puerto Rico.

In Las Vegas, as long as the dice stay on the table, the roll is good no matter where they happen to stop—even if one or both are leaning against some object (in the case of leaners, the side of the die with the highest elevation is used). But in Puerto Rico, where gambling is controlled by the government, a string is stretched across the center of the table and unless the dice come to rest between the string and the backboard the roll does not count. There, any roll that is even a shade less than orthodox can initiate a shouting match between players and housemen and players and players that necessitates calling in the government inspectors for arbitration.

The first roll is called the "come-out" roll. When the dice stop, two sets of dots will be showing on top. Added together, the number of dots that are showing constitute the "number" the shooter has rolled. For instance, if two dots are showing on one die and six dots are showing on the other die, the shooter has rolled an eight.

If the shooter is betting with the dice (as most but not all shooters do), he will hope—possibly even pray—that he will throw a seven or an eleven on the come-out. Should he be so fortunate as to do so, he has rolled a "natural," and has become an instant winner. He will retain the dice and repeat the process of betting and throwing another come-out roll.

On the other hand, the shooter is equally hopeful on the come-out roll that he will not throw a two

(two ones—"snake-eyes"), a three (a two and a one —"acey-deucey"), or a twelve (two sixes—"box-cars"). If he does he will have rolled "craps," and immediately relegated himself to the vastly over-crowded ranks of the losers. He will **not** lose the dice, but having lost his bet on craps, he will have to make a new bet before throwing another come-out roll.

Let's assume, though, that the shooter neither craps out nor throws a natural on the initial roll, but, instead, rolls one of the other possible num-bers—four, five, six, eight, nine or ten. That num-ber becomes his "point." He then continues to throw the dice. If he rolls his point again before he rolls a seven, he wins. But if the seven comes up first, he loses—he has "sevened out." Now, he must relinquish the dice.

(Note that on the come-out, for the bettor who is betting with the dice, the seven wins for him, but when he is rolling for a point, the seven loses for him. It can lead to deeply ambivalent feelings about sevens.)

To repeat:

If the shooter who is betting with the dice rolls a seven or an eleven on the come-out, he wins.

If the shooter rolls a two, three or twelve on the come-out, he loses.

If the shooter rolls a point number and then rolls that point number again before he rolls a seven, he wins.

If the shooter rolls a point number and then rolls a seven before he rolls the point number again, he loses.

Basically, that is the game.

BETTING

There is, of course, more to the game than the basics. What those many different sections on the layout mean is that the players are offered a variety of ways to bet. There are more ways, in fact, than there are sections on the layout; ways that we will discuss when we get to taking and giving odds and buying numbers.

Craps players appreciate this variety because it makes the game more interesting and gives them, they think, additional ways to win. The house is happy to accommodate this desire for a multitude of chances because it actually provides the casino with additional opportunities to rake in the players' money. For the players, variety is the spice of life. For the house, that translates as: There is more than one way to skin a sucker.

Let's consider the various bets. Here we'll be concerned only with the mechanics of making the bets. The odds and percentages that make them good bets or bad bets will be covered in the next chapter.

Pass Line Bet

A **pass** line bettor is betting with the dice and is called a "right" bettor. He wins when the come-out roll produces a seven or an eleven (natural) and loses when a two, three or twelve is thrown (craps). Or, if neither a natural nor craps is rolled on the come-out, the **pass** line bettor wins when the shooter rolls his point and loses when the shooter rolls a seven before making his point (sevens out).

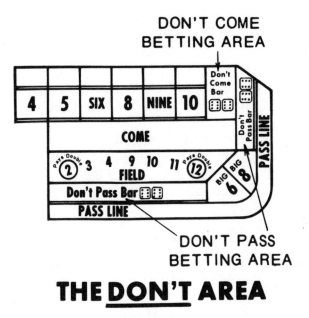

DON'T COME
BETTING AREA

DON'T PASS
BETTING AREA

THE <u>DON'T</u> AREA

A **don't pass** bettor is betting against the dice. He is the opposite of the **pass** bettor, in that he is called a "wrong" bettor and his bet is a "wrong" bet, whereas the pass bettor is called a "right" bettor and his bet is a "right" bet. Simply, the **pass** or right bettor bets that the dice will do what the shooter wants them to do, and the **don't pass** or wrong bettor bets that they won't.

If the shooter rolls craps on the come-out, the **don't pass** bettor wins—unless. Unless the number happens to be twelve (or, in some cases, two). The wording on the **don't pass** section will be: Don't Pass Bar Twelve (or Two). This means that the twelve (or two) is withheld—for the reason that if it weren't, the advantage would not be sufficiently in favor of the casino. The casino, you may be sure, is no fool. Some casinos bar the twelve, some bar the two. If the barred number is rolled it is neutral for the **don't pass** bettor; that is, it has no effect on his bet. The house edge is that the casino, paying nothing to the wrong bettors, wins the right bettors' money.

If on the come-out roll the shooter throws a seven or eleven (natural), the **don't pass** bettor loses.

If the shooter rolls neither a natural nor craps on the come-out and then begins shooting to make his point, the **don't pass** bettor wins if the shooter sevens out, and loses if the shooter makes his point.[1]

Come Bet

A **come** bettor is a right bettor. A **come** bet can be made only after a point has been established. But, no matter at what point in the game a player makes a **come** bet, the next roll of the dice for him is a come-out roll.

If a player makes a **come** bet and a seven or eleven is thrown on the next roll, he wins. If craps (two, three or twelve) is rolled, he loses.

So far, the **come** bet is the same as the **pass** line bet. But if a point number (four, five, six, eight, nine, ten) is rolled, the **come** bet ceases to follow the pattern of the **pass** line bet.

[1] Note: There are some players who, when they are shooters, will bet against the dice, making **don't pass** bets, their theory being that they are unlucky shooters. That does not affect the game for the other bettors, though. If a seven is rolled on the come-out, for instance, even though the shooter, betting against the dice, will lose his own bet, the right bettors will still win.

This is what happens:

The bet in the **come** box is moved to the point number in the section where the **place** bets are made (see layout, p. 38, directly above the **come** section), and the player can now make a new **come** bet. For the **come** bettor the next roll of the dice will be both a new come-out roll (on his new **come** bet) and a second roll (on his bet on the point number). In effect, the **come** bettor is starting a different game all his own, each roll increasing his action.

Let's follow a series of bets to show how it works. We'll call our player Mr. Right, for the reason that he is a right bettor.

On the come-out roll the shooter rolls a nine. Since he has neither crapped out and lost nor thrown a natural and won, he retains the dice and continues to shoot, hoping to roll a nine, his point.

Mr. Right has made a **pass** line bet, so his point, too, is nine. Now, he also makes a **come** bet. He does this by placing chips (his bet) on the **come** section of the layout.

On the next throw the shooter rolls a four. He is not affected (he has neither made his point, nine, nor sevened out). Similarly, Mr. Right's **pass** line bet is not affected. For the **come** bet, though, there is action. The chips that Mr. Right put on the **come** section are now moved to the four box on the layout. So, in this private game that Mr. Right is playing, he now has two point numbers—nine and four. Again he places a bet on the **come** section.

On the next throw, the shooter rolls a six. He is still not affected. There is no effect on Mr. Right's **pass** line bet nor on his bet in the four box. But the bet that he placed in the **come** section the second time is now moved to the six box. His points now are nine, four and six. Once more he makes a new **come** bet.

The shooter, throwing again, rolls a four. He is still not affected. Four, though, is one of Mr. Right's points, so he collects. The dealer hands him his bet and his winnings from the four box and they are replaced by the bet from the **come** section. Again his points are nine (**pass** line bet), six and four. He makes a new **come** bet.

The shooter rolls a three. Since his point is nine and he is not affected by craps when he is rolling for a point, he still is neither a winner nor a loser. Mr. Right's bets on nine, six and four are not affected either by craps. On the **come** bet, however, the throw was a come-out roll, and since craps was rolled he is a loser. The dealer removes his chips from the **come** section. Mr. Right's points are still nine (on the **pass** line), six and four, and he makes another new **come** bet.

On the subsequent three throws, the shooter rolls a six, a four and an eight. As far as he is concerned nothing has happened. Mr. Right, however, collects on the four and the six, both of which are his points, and his winnings are replaced by bets made in the **come** section. A bet from the **come** section is also moved to the number eight box. At this juncture, his points are nine (**pass** line), six, four and eight, and he has made a new **come** bet.

The shooter rolls a seven. He loses, he has sevened out. Because a seven has been rolled before any of his point numbers, Mr. Right loses on the nine (**pass** line), six, four and eight. But he wins on the **come** bet, for the reason that the throw on that bet was a new come-out roll, and the seven represented a natural.

It is the hope of the **come** bettor, of course, that

the shooter will continue to shoot for a long while, rolling the numbers on which the **come** bettor has money and avoiding sevening out. Needless to say, it doesn't always happen that way. Often, as soon as the **come** bettor gets all set up with the bets on all of the numbers the shooter rolls a seven and the come bettor is immediately wiped out.

Don't Come Bet

The **don't come** bet is to the **come** bet what the **don't pass** bet is to the **pass** bet—almost exactly the opposite. The shading of difference is that—as in the case of the **don't pass** bet—a win on the two or the twelve is withheld from the **don't pass** bettor, while neither is barred as a loss to the **come** bettor.

The **don't come** bettor is a wrong bettor, betting against the dice, hoping that the dice will not do what the shooter wants them to do.

As we did with Mr. Right, our **come** bettor, let's tag along with Mr. Wrong, a **don't come** bettor, through a series of rolls and see what happens: Being a wrong bettor, Mr. Wrong makes a **don't pass** bet prior to the come-out. Then on the come-out the shooter rolls a six. Six becomes the shooter's point. It also becomes the **don't** point for Mr. Wrong, the point he does not want the shooter to roll again before he sevens out. He now places a bet on the **don't come** section (see figure p. 45).

On the next throw, the shooter rolls a four. Since he has not made his point, six, nor sevened out, he is not affected. There is no effect either on Mr. Wrong's **don't pass** bet. His **don't come** bet, however, is now moved to the four box (placed in the half-box section just above the whole box in which the number appears). He is betting that a seven will come up before a four (and, on the **don't pass** bet, that a seven will come up before a six, the shooter's point). He places another bet on the **don't come** section.

The shooter, throwing again, rolls a five. He is not affected—nor is Mr. Wrong's **don't pass** bet. Mr. Wrong's **don't come** bet is moved to the five box. He is now betting that a seven will come up before a six (on the **don't pass** bet) or a four or a five repeats. And he makes another **don't come** bet.

The shooter rolls another four. He is still not affected. Mr. Wrong loses the bet on the four box (because the number was repeated before a seven came up). It is replaced by the chips resting on the **don't come** section and a new **don't come** bet is made.

The shooter rolls again and sevens out. Mr. Wrong collects on the **don't pass** bet and on the number four and number five bets (because the seven came up before the numbers were repeated). He loses on the bet in the **don't come** section because, for him, the throw was a come-out roll and the seven represented a natural.

Clearly, the **don't come** bettor, like the **don't pass** bettor, hopes that the dice will be "cold"—that is, wrong. For if he has **don't come** bets on several numbers, a seven can make him a substantial winner.

Place Bet

Let's look at the layout again (see p. 38). Those boxes with the numbers in them, located just above the **come** section, are for making **place** bets. They were used also as part of the process of making **come** bets.

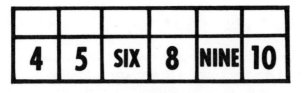

THE NUMBERS AREA

To get a bet into the boxes with a **come** bet it is necessary to place it first on the **come** section and then wait for the number to be rolled. The **place** bettor, though, ignores the **come** section. He places his bet on any number—four, five, six, eight, nine or ten—in the **place** section at any time he wants to do so after the come-out roll. Normally, a **place** bettor will make a pass line bet prior to the come-out.

The **place** bettor is betting that the shooter will roll his (the **place** bettor's) number or numbers before he rolls a seven. A **place** bet is affected **only** when the place bettor's number or numbers are rolled or when the shooter throws a seven.

Here is how it works:

On the come-out the shooter rolls a five. That is his point. Since the **place** bettor has made a **pass** line bet, five is also his point. He now makes **place** bets on the other point numbers—four, six, eight, nine and ten.

On succeeding throws, the shooter rolls eight, two, six, nine, four, eleven, five, nine, eight, four, three, six, five, two, eight, ten, ten, four, twelve, six and seven.

Note that on the seventh roll after the come-out the shooter made his point, five, and collected.

Having made a **pass** line bet, the **place** bettor also collected when the shooter made the point. Both the shooter and the **place** bettor then made a new **pass** line bet.

The next roll, a nine, was a new come-out roll, and on come-out rolls the **place** bets are "frozen"; that is, they remain where they are and are not affected by the roll. For the **place** bettor the number five was no longer covered, so his **place** bet on the nine was moved, at his request, to the number five, for the reason that he had the nine—the shooter's new point—covered by his new **pass** line bet and saw no reason for having double coverage on the number.

In all, the **place** bettor collected on fifteen of the rolls. On five of the throws—when two, three, eleven and twelve were rolled—the **place** bettor was not affected. And finally when the shooter rolled a seven, the **place** bets were all lost.

Pleasant thought, isn't it, winning on all of those rolls? But let's examine a different series of throws:

On the come-out, the shooter rolls a five. That is his point. It is also the **place** bettor's point, since he has made a **pass** line bet. The **place** bettor now makes bets on all of the additional point numbers —four, six, eight, nine and ten.

On the next roll, the shooter rolls a seven.

The **place** bettor is wiped out. His **pass** line bet is lost because the shooter sevened out. And his **place** bets are lost because a seven came up before any of the numbers were rolled.

What the **place** bettor is hoping for is that the shooter will roll a long string of numbers and avoid like the plague throwing a seven.

In fact, contrary to popular belief, it is not a natural on a come-out roll that excites craps shooters;

it is a long string of numbers. That is what makes a table hot; that is when the big money can be won. It is called—appropriately enough—"rolling numbers." At a casino when you see a great number of customers suddenly converging on a certain table it is probably because word has spread that the shooter at that table is "rolling numbers." The newcomers want to take advantage of the hot roll —making **place** bets—before it cools off.

Field Bet

Field bets are made on that large section of the layout that has the word "field" and a variety of numbers on it. The numbers are different at different casinos, but, to illustrate, let's say that they are two, three, four, nine, ten, eleven and twelve, with the numbers two and twelve circled.

A **field** bet is a one-roll bet. Every time the dice are thrown, the **field** bets are decided; they win or lose. **Field** bets can be made at any time during the game, on the come-out or any subsequent roll. When you bet on the field, you are covered on **all** of the numbers. If the throw produces a two, three, four, nine, ten, eleven or twelve, the **field** bettor wins—no matter what happens to the shooter. If any other number comes up—five, six, seven or eight—the **field** bettor loses—again, regardless of the effect on the shooter.

The circles around the two and twelve indicate that the house pays double on those numbers. That is, if the **field** bettor puts a five-dollar bet on the field and the two or twelve is rolled, he is paid not even money, five dollars, as on the uncircled numbers, but double, ten dollars.

At first glance, the **field** has all the aspects of the Elysian Fields. There are all of those winning numbers, two, three, four, nine, ten, eleven and twelve—and, to boot, a double payoff on the two and twelve—and so few losing numbers, only five, six, seven and eight.

That's what the casino wants the player to think: that he has discovered gamblers' heaven. That is why the **field** is so prominent on the layout. And it is not simply by chance that the stickman keeps urging the bettors to "play the **field**."

In fact, because of the odds, which we will discuss in the next chapter, a **field** bet is one of the worst bets on the table.

Big 6 And Big 8

The **Big 6 And Big 8** section also stands out on the table like a prostitute waving a red lantern. And for the same reason: to attract customers.

The **Big 6 And Big 8** bettor is betting that the shooter will roll a six or an eight before he rolls a seven. If the six or eight comes up first, he wins; if the seven comes up first, he loses.

At this point we have discussed all of the obvious bets that can bo made on the wings of the layout—**pass** line, **don't pass** line, **come, don't come, place, field** and **Big 6 And Big 8**. Now let's examine the bets that are available to the player on the square in the center of the layout. These are **any seven** bets, **hardways, proposition** bets and **any craps**. With the exception of the **hardways,** they are all one-roll bets.

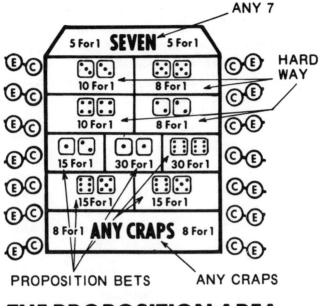

PROPOSITION BETS   ANY CRAPS

THE PROPOSITION AREA

Hardways

Rolling a number the hard way means to roll it by throwing a particular combination of two pairs of other numbers. On a **hardways** bet, the specific numbers and combinations are: the number four by rolling a pair of twos; the number six by rolling a pair of threes; the number eight by rolling a pair of fours; and the number ten by rolling a pair of fives. The term **hardways** is appropriate because it's a hell of a hard way to roll a number.

When a player makes a **hardways** bet he is facing double jeopardy. If a seven comes up before the **hardways** combination he has bet, he loses. He also loses if the number he has bet comes up as a different combination—if, for example, the shooter rolls a four with a combination of three and one; or a six with a combination of one and five or two and four; or an eight with a combination of two and six or three and five; or a ten with a combination of four and six.

Think about it.

Any Seven

A one-roll bet. The player is betting that on the next throw of the dice the shooter will roll a seven. If the seven comes up, the bettor wins. If any other number is rolled, the bettor loses.

Propositions

The **proposition** is another one-roll bet. The numbers that can be bet are two, three, eleven and twelve. The player can bet any or all of these numbers and is betting that on the next roll of the dice the number or numbers he has bet will come up. If he is correct, he wins; if not, he loses.

Any Craps

Any craps is still another one-roll bet. The player bets all three of the numbers that normally constitute craps—two, three and twelve—with one bet. If on the next roll of the dice, any one of these numbers is thrown, the bettor wins. Conversely, if any of the many other numbers comes up, the bettor loses.

There are three additional bets that can usually be made. They are the **turn** (or **hop**) bet, the **eleven** bet and the **horn** bet.

When the shooter is rolling for a point, a **turn**, or **hop**, bet is made on the next roll (turn or hop) of the dice. The player bets that the point number will come up as a particular combination. Let's say the point is nine. The **turn** bettor will call out, "Forty-five on the turn," and make his bet. This means that he is betting that the point number, nine, will be made on the next roll of the dice in the form of a four and a five. If that happens, he wins. If another number comes up, or if the point number is rolled as a different combination (six and three, for instance), he loses.

In actual fact, a **turn** bet can be made on any roll. But it is the usual practice to make it when a shooter is rolling for a point. The purpose is to "root the number home." **Turn** bettors evidently believe that a **turn** bet can influence the dice. Nonsense.

The **eleven** bettor calls out "Yo 'leven," and makes his bet. He is betting that the eleven will come up on the next roll. If it does, he wins; if it doesn't, he loses.

The **horn** bet (in Puerto Rico, called "Santurce") is a bit more complicated. The bettor is betting a certain amount of money, which is spread over certain combinations of numbers. Let's say that the bet is five dollars. One dollar would be allocated to the combination of a pair of ones, one dollar to a pair of sixes, one dollar to a one and a two, and two dollars to the eleven. If one of those combinations comes up, the bettor wins that segment of the bet. If anything else comes up, he loses.

We have now discussed the equipment and the mechanics of making the bets that are displayed on the layout. But that is only the start. For it is the subtleties—knowing and understanding the odds and percentages and knowing how to use these and other factors to your advantage—that separate the winners from the losers.

THE MATHEMATICS

In ancient days it was believed that dice, along with everything else, were controlled by the gods. Somewhere, I imagine, there is a craps player who still believes that. I base this assumption on the fact that I know there are craps players who honestly think they can affect the roll of the dice by talking to them, as if those little plastic cubes had ears and a brain and a compassionate, or possibly larcenous, heart.

Mathematicians, however, have demonstrated that the gods have nothing to do with it. The gods are all busy choosing up sides for whatever war or football game is going on at the moment. When it comes to craps they couldn't be less interested. What **does** make a difference is the odds. And for both the players and the casino owners that is probably just as well. For gods are notoriously capricious. But odds are constant. Thus the players, who **should** know the odds, and the casino owners, who **do** know the odds, have the opportunity to know what to expect.

ODDS

Odds are based on the theory of probability, which tells us what will **probably** happen in a given situation when some of the factors that affect that situation are known and others remain unknown.

In craps, probability tells us how often any certain combination of numbers will probably be thrown. The lowest probability is zero, which means that a certain result cannot possibly happen. For an illustration of probability zero, try rolling a thirteen with a pair of dice. The highest probability, on the other hand, is one, which means that a particular result is certain to occur. It is a certainty, for example, when you roll a pair of dice, that the number that comes up will be between two and twelve.

To show in the simplest way how probabilities are translated into odds, let's use the common practice of tossing a coin. The factor that is known is that there are two sides to the coin, heads and tails. A factor that is not known is how much force the tosser will use when throwing the coin into the air. What we know, then, is that the coin will come down either heads or tails. Based on that, the probability that it will come down heads is equal to the probability that it will come down tails. The odds, consequently, are even (equal).

In craps, though, we use two dice. Each die has

six sides, and each side has a different number—
one, two, three, four, five or six. And, together,
these numbers can add up to eleven different combinations, two, three, four, five, six, seven, eight,
nine, ten, eleven or twelve.

Additionally, there are more than eleven ways
of rolling these numbers. A nine, for example, can
be rolled with four different combinations: three
and six (three on die "A"; six on die "B"), six and
three (six on die "A"; three on die "B"), four and
five, and five and four. There are six ways that a
seven can be thrown; one and six, six and one,
two and five, five and two, three and four, and four
and three. Only the two (one and one) and the
twelve (six and six) are limited to a single possibility.

Clearly, the probability that a nine will be rolled
is not the same as the probability that a seven will
be rolled. And, just as obviously, the probability of
a seven coming up is different than the probability
that a two or twelve will be thrown.

All in all, there are thirty-six possible combinations. As follows:

Number	Combinations	Ways
2	1-1	1
3	1-2, 2-1	2
4	1-3, 3-1, 2-2	3
5	1-4, 4-1, 2-3, 3-2	4
6	1-5, 5-1, 2-4, 4-2, 3-3	5
7	1-6, 6-1, 2-5, 5-2, 3-4, 4-3	6
8	2-6, 6-2, 3-5, 5-3, 4-4	5
9	3-6, 6-3, 4-5, 5-4	4
10	4-6, 6-4, 5-5	3
11	5-6, 6-5	2
12	6-6	1
	Total	36

With this scale to work with, we can now figure out what the odds are for any number that can be rolled with a pair of dice.

Here is how the odds are calculated:

There is only one way out of a possible thirty-six that a twelve can be thrown—by rolling a pair of sixes. Thus when the dice are thrown there is one chance (probability) that they will come up twelve and thirty-five chances that they won't. **Odds are the unfavorable probabilities as opposed to the favorable probabilities.** So the odds **against** rolling a twelve are thirty-five probabilities to one probability—or, thirty-five to one.

Let's look at the odds for the seven. There are six combinations that make up this number. So when the dice are thrown there are six probabilities that a seven will be rolled and thirty probabilities that it won't. The odds, therefore, are thirty to six (or, broken down, five to one) against rolling a seven.

As the probabilities change, the odds change.

Let's take a look now at the odds on all of the numbers that can be rolled:

As mentioned, the odds on twelve are thirty-five to one. The same applies to the two, which also can be rolled in only one way (two ones); the odds on two, similarly, are thirty-five to one. The odds against throwing a three or an eleven (both of which can be made two ways) are thirty-four to two, or seventeen to one. And the odds on seven, as noted previously, are five to one.

That covers the odds on the numbers that can win or lose for the player on the come-out roll—seven and eleven, naturals, and two, three and twelve, craps.

The odds on the point numbers, four, five, six,

eight, nine and ten are, of course, computed differently, since you're not betting here on your number versus all the other possible combinations which can be made with a pair of dice. You're merely betting that your point number will be rolled before one other number: the killer, the seven. Thus, if, for example, your point number is four (which can be rolled three ways: with a one on die "A" and a three on die "B," or a three on die "A" and a one on die "B," or a two on die "A" and a two on die "B") and there are six ways to roll a seven, the odds against a four—the odds that a seven will be rolled before a four is rolled—are six to three, or, stated in reduced form, two to one. These, then, are the true odds on all point numbers:

Number	Odds
4	two to one
5	three to two
6	six to five
8	six to five
9	three to two
10	two to one

PERCENTAGE

For a gambling casino to stay in business it must take in more money than it pays out. It accomplishes this noble capitalistic purpose by using the odds to its own advantage, by paying off the winners at a figure that is less than the true odds on the bet. The spread between the true odds and the odds that the house pays is the percentage (called P.C.)—the percentage in the casino's favor.

For example, let's say that a player makes an **any seven** bet. On the next roll, a seven is thrown. Since the odds are five to one against a seven coming up, the house, theoretically, should pay off at that rate, five to one. In fact, however, the player is paid off at four to one. The difference between the theoretical payoff and the actual pay-off is the percentage, the casino's profit.

Because the odds are different on different bets, the casino's percentage, of course, varies too. On the **any seven** bet described above, the house's percentage is 16.7. On a **Big 6 And Big 8** bet, paying even money, the house has an 8.09 percent advantage. And the casino's percentage on an **any craps** bet that pays seven to one is 11.1. Over all, the casino's advantage ranges from a low of .83 to a high of 16.7.

Note that although the percentage varies from bet to bet it is always with the casino; it is never with the player. There is absolutely nothing any player can do on any single roll of the dice (short of cheating) to transfer the advantage from the house to himself. The **best** a player can do is reduce the casino's percentage to the minimum over a poriod of time.

Reducing the house's advantage to the minimum is one of the several factors that contribute to making a player a winner. The reason is this: The dice do not perform on every series of rolls exactly as the probabilities dictate. There are periods when the house is winning and periods when the house is losing. Over the long haul, the house will win. Nevertheless, those periods when it is losing do exist. At times, in fact, it seems as if those capricious gods have more to do with how the dice come up than the theory of probabilities.

For instance, if a shooter throws the dice six

times there is no absolute certainty that a seven will come up once and some other number will come up the other five times—even though the odds are five to one. For the theory of probabilities, as it relates to craps and rolling a seven, is not based on a six-roll series. It is based on eternity. So, although if a player stuck around for eternity, playing craps twenty-four hours a day, he would roll five other numbers for every seven that came up, the same odds would not necessarily hold for a six-roll series. In the six rolls, the shooter might roll two sevens or four sevens or even six sevens—any number of times from zero to six.

When these disruptions in what is generally thought to be the normal pattern of the theory of probabilities occur, the dice are said to be "hot" or "cold." When the shooter is rolling winning number after winning number for the right bettors, the dice are hot. When, as has been known to happen, the shooter is rolling losing number after losing number for the right bettors, the dice are cold.

The inference that can be drawn from this is that craps is a right-bettor's world. If that world were shared equally with the wrong bettors, who bet against the dice, the dice would also be said to be hot when they were producing losing number after losing number for the right bettors, making winners of the wrong bettors. But such is not the case. The dice are hot only when they are winning for the right bettors. It is discrimination, no doubt about it, and a cause that the wrong bettors of the world might want to take up.

TAKING AND GIVING ODDS

Remember: the best a player can do is reduce the house's advantage to the minimum over a period of time.

One of the ways a player can do this is by taking or giving the odds. This can be done on **pass** and **don't pass** bets, and on **come** and **don't come** bets after they have been moved to the box numbers. Players "take" the odds on **pass** and **come** bets, and "give" or "lay" the odds on **don't pass** and **don't come** bets.

You will find no section on the layout for taking or giving odds. That is because just as the casino goes out of its way to advertise a bet like **Big 6 And Big 8,** which provides the house with a large advantage, it does its best to ignore the bettor's option to take or give odds, which has the effect of lowering the casino's percentage.

The player takes or gives odds by increasing his bet. On **pass** line bets, the additional chips are placed directly behind the first bet (and called a "back bet"). On **don't pass** bets the extra chips are placed next to the first bet. On **come** bets, the odds chips are placed on top of the first bet, but slightly out of line so that it can be seen that they are separate. On a **don't come** bet the odds bet is placed alongside the original bet (and if an additional odds bet is made it is placed like a bridge across the first two stacks of chips).

Here is how it works in play. Let's assume that you bet ten dollars on the **pass** line. You are a right bettor, betting that the dice will pass (win). On the come-out roll the shooter throws a ten (six and four). The odds against a shooter rolling a ten again and making his point before a seven comes up are two to one.

You now take the odds, increasing your bet by an equivalent amount; in this case, ten dollars. The odds bet is placed directly behind the initial bet. On this back bet the house gives two to one odds. Thus the house's percentage is reduced. For, instead of having the opportunity to win ten dollars with a ten-dollar bet (the **pass** line bet at even money), you now have the chance to win thirty dollars on a twenty-dollar bet (ten dollars on the **pass** line bet, plus twenty dollars on the back bet, which pays two to one).

When you made the **pass** line bet, the casino's advantage against you was 1.41 percent. By making the odds bet, you brought the house's percentage down to .84.

In the example used above, the initial bet was increased by the equivalent amount—a **pass** line bet of ten dollars and a back bet of ten dollars. Although it is general practice for bettors to make odds bets in amounts that are the same as the original bet, it is not mandatory in all cases. The amount can always be for less or, in a few rare instances, specifically when the point is five, six, eight or nine, for more.

Here is how it works when it is for more:

The odds on the six or eight are six to five. Let's say that you bet fifteen dollars (three five-dollar chips) on the **pass** line and take the odds with the same amount—fifteen dollars—on the back bet and win. To pay off at the six to five ratio, the house would have to give you eighteen dollars for the fifteen-dollar back bet. That would require using one-dollar chips. To simplify the transaction for the dealer, the house prefers to pay off in the same units that the bettor is using. That is, if you are betting with five-dollar chips, the house likes to pay off with five-dollar chips.

So, even though you have only fifteen dollars on the **pass** line, the house allows you to make a back bet of twenty-five dollars. The mathematics involved if you win are elementary. The five units (five chips) are paid off with six units (six chips, or thirty dollars).

You can take advantage of this deviation from the norm, though, only if your bet is three units or more. The reason for this is that the house is giving you a definite leverage and so it wants to make sure that your bet is for a reasonable amount, three five-dollar chips or more.

Now, having advised you of the rule, I must add that it doesn't always hold. You **can** bet in between as well—for instance, four five-dollar chips, twenty dollars, in back of your fifteen-dollar bet on the six or eight. The payoff on that—at six to five—is twenty-four dollars.

Similarly, if you are using ten-dollar units, and you have, say, thirty dollars on the line, you can make an odds bet of forty or forty-five dollars— you are not confined to betting only fifty dollars (five units on which the house can make an easy payoff of six units or sixty dollars).

The house's rationale is that as long as it is allowing you to bet more, it must continue with the liberality, letting you bet whatever you want to in between and not limiting you to the preferred five-unit bet. You could make, for example, a thirty-eight-dollar bet. What the dealer would do in such a case would be to pay off at six to five to the nearest divisible amount, and even money after that. Since thirty-eight is not divisible by five or six, the dealer would divide to the nearest figure. Five into thirty-five goes seven times, and six times seven is forty-two. So he would pay off the thirty-five dollars of your thirty-eight-dollar bet with forty-two dollars, and give you three more dollars for your remaining three dollars, a payoff of forty-five dollars for your thirty-eight.

It is a bad idea to make this kind of bet, however, for the reason that you are cheating yourself by allowing the house to pay off part of your bet with even money instead of odds. Here is what I mean: On that portion of your bet that is divisible by five (thirty-five dollars), the house is paying you the correct odds of six to five. For the remaining three dollars of your bet, though, the house is paying you only even money, which makes that portion as much of a sucker bet as **Big 6 And Big 8.** So, you are far better off making your odds bets in amounts divisible by five—forty, forty-five or fifty dollars. In this way you get full six to five odds for every dollar you invest (forty-eight dollars on a forty-dollar bet, fifty-four dollars on a forty-five dollar bet, sixty dollars on a fifty-dollar bet).

The same opportunity is open to you on the five and nine. Since the correct odds payoff on these numbers is three to two, the house prefers to simplify its payoffs, and will let you make a larger odds bet than your line bet if the amount of your line bet is not divisible by two. Let's say that your line bet is fifteen dollars. Since fifteen is not divisible by two, this will give the house mathematical headaches if you also make an odds bet of fifteen dollars—and it will be a foolish bet for you because you will get only even money on that part of your bet that doesn't divide. On fifteen dollars, the house would pay you odds on that part of the bet that does divide (fourteen dollars), with the result that your payoff at three to two would get you twenty-one dollars for your fourteen dollars. On the leftover dollar, of course, you get only even money, one dollar for one dollar, whereas, at three to two odds, you really should get one dollar and fifty cents for your one dollar. By not receiving full payment, you are making a gift to the house of fifty percent of your original one-dollar investment, forfeiting the fifty cents of the dollar and a half that you should have been paid.

For this reason, and to save themselves the trouble of complicated mathematics, the house will let you bet up to the next "round" even amount for your odds bet—that is, for example, a twenty-dollar odds bet if your line bet is fifteen dollars. Thus you have the same opportunity, as with the six and eight, of making a more conservative bet on the line, and a bigger one for the odds bet with its nice payoff. (To summarize: If you bet fifteen dollars on your line bet, you get back fifteen dollars. If you then bet twenty dollars on your odds bet, you get back thirty dollars, meaning a return of forty-five dollars on your thirty-five-dollar investment.)

Obviously, you can achieve an even amount on the odds bet, when your line bet is fifteen dollars, by making the odds bet sixteen dollars—which is divisible by two, and on which the payoff would be twenty-four dollars. But why do it? That is just being nice to the house. It is limiting one of the few bets on which the house is obligated to pay full odds. So, bet the maximum amount, such as twenty dollars on a fifteen-dollar line bet, and get back thirty dollars if you win.

Taking advantage of this flexible method of odds betting is especially important to the player with tight money. He is betting a conservative bet on the **pass** line because that is an even-money bet and he is running a risk of getting knocked off by a craps. Then, if a five, six, eight or nine appears, he can make a bigger bet as the back bet—since he is getting a bargain, full odds without paying "vigorish" for it.

In the past, many casinos allowed players double odds—that is, an odds bet in an amount double the line bet—reducing the house's advantage even more. There are still at this writing a few casinos in the Downtown section of Las Vegas that allow double odds, but for the most part the advantage has gone the way of the one-hundred-cent dollar.

The process of giving the odds is essentially the same as taking the odds. The differences are that it is wrong bettors who give the odds (on **don't pass** and **don't come** bets), and that the percentages are not exactly the same. Giving odds, the **don't pass** and **don't come** bettor can reduce the house's advantage against him from 1.40 to .83 percent.

The advantage is still against the bettor, of course. There is no possible way that the bettor can reduce the house's advantage to zero or acquire the advantage for himself. As you can see, though, by taking or giving the odds the bettor can substantially reduce the casino's percentage and thus increase his own chances of winning.

The following table shows exactly how the house's percentage is lowered when the player exercises his option to bet the odds.

Bet	Payoff	P.C.
pass	even money	1.41
pass + odds	even money + odds	.84
don't pass	even money	1.40
don't pass + odds	even money + odds	.83
come	even money	1.41
come + odds	even money + odds	.84
don't come	even money	1.40
don't come + odds	even money + odds	.83

BUYING THE NUMBER

Buying the number relates to **place** bets—bets on the point numbers (four, five, six, eight, nine and ten) in the boxes. When a player makes a **place** bet, he gets the odds that the house offers—nine to five on the four or ten; seven to five on the five or nine; and seven to six on the six or eight.

When the player buys the number he makes a **place** bet, pays a fee (vigorish), and gets the real odds on the number as opposed to the odds the house normally gives. The dealer places a "buy tag" (a small plastic disc) on the bet and calls out loudly, "Vig paid!" The shout is to notify his employers that the fee, a kind of **quid pro quo** for the reduction of the house's advantage, has been collected.

The fee is five percent of the amount of the bet. Since the smallest denomination used in most casinos is one dollar, the bet on which the player buys the number should not be for less than twenty dollars (one dollar is five percent of twenty dollars). The odds the player gets after buying the number are: two to one on the four or ten; three to two on the five or nine; and six to five on the six or eight.

This is what it looks like in table form:

Number	Actual Odds	House Odds
4 or 10	two to one	nine to five
5 or 9	three to two	seven to five
6 or 8	six to five	seven to six

Here is how the play goes:

You make a twenty-dollar **place** bet on number four and buy the number, paying the dealer a five percent fee of one dollar. For this fee you get two to one odds on the number four instead of the usual odds of nine to five.

The dice are rolled and the number four comes up. At two to one odds, you collect forty dollars. Since you paid a one-dollar fee, your bet actually produces thirty-nine dollars.

Let's compare that with a conventional **place** bet on number four. You make a twenty-dollar wager. The dice are rolled and the number four comes up. In this instance, the house plays nine to five odds and you collect thirty-six dollars. This is three dollars less than you would have won if you had bought the number.

Three dollars, by itself, is not a magnificent sum, granted. But, remember, you risked only one dollar to win the three dollars. Three for one is an attractive profit margin in any business transaction. During a night of play, with a new roll being thrown every few seconds, the additional dividends can add up to a hefty sum. They can, in fact, constitute a substantial share of a player's winnings. When the table is hot and the player is collecting consistently on a three-for-one basis, his stake can quickly produce a profit amounting to thousands of dollars. So, under the right conditions, this can be the best bet on the table.

Since the odds on the five and nine and the six and eight are different from the odds on the four and ten, the result when buying the five or nine or six or eight are also different.

Let's say that you buy either the five or nine, making a twenty-dollar bet and paying a one-dollar fee. A win will produce thirty dollars. Subtract the one-dollar fee for buying the number and the net is twenty-nine dollars. If you had made a simple **place** bet on five or nine and received the house odds of seven to five, a win would have given you twenty-eight dollars.

In this instance, the spread between the twenty-nine-dollar win in the one case and the twenty-eight-dollar win in the other is so small that it is outweighed by the fact that you had to risk more money to win more money. In other words, it costs a dollar for the chance to gain a dollar. In percentage figures, it cost you four percent to **place** the number and five percent to buy the number. So, by buying, you increased your disadvantage.

When you buy the six or eight the same thing happens as when you buy the five or nine—you pay for the dubious privilege of making it easier for the house to beat you.

WORKING AND NOT WORKING

You will hear the term "working" used at the crap table quite a bit. A bet will be said to be working or not working. That simply means that the bet is either in play (working) or not in play (not working). Some bets can be removed after they have been made or can be suspended for a roll or two, even though they have not been physically removed from the table. And some bets are automatically suspended for a period of one roll.

Line bets—**pass** line and **don't pass** line—are always working. Once made, they cannot be removed or suspended. The same applies to the come bet, while it is on the come section and after it has been moved to a box number.

Odds wagers on these bets, though, are different. Odds bets on **pass** and **don't pass** bets can be removed at any time. The odds bets on come bets that have been moved to the boxes are automatically "off" (not working) on a come-out roll. Therefore, on a come-out roll if a come bettor's number is rolled, he is paid on the come bet but not on the odds bet. And if a seven is rolled he loses his come bet but not his odds bet (the odds bet is handed back to him).

Place bets and such bets as **hardways** (bets that are not one-roll bets) can also be removed or suspended at any time. If the player wants to freeze them, he says to the dealer, "**Off** next roll (or next two rolls or whatever) on my bets." The dealer will place a small disc—marked "Off"—on the bets. If discs are not used, the dealer will move the bets to the lines that separate the sections. If the player wants the bets removed permanently, he says to the dealer, "**Down** on my bets," and the bets are removed and handed to him.

As I mentioned earlier, on the come-out roll, some bets, like the odds on the come bets, are automatically frozen. A player can unfreeze them, however, by saying to the dealer, "My odds work on the come-out." Few players do this, though. Because on a come-out roll the majority of the players at the table, being right bettors, are rooting for a seven, and most bettors, being somewhat superstitious, prefer not to buck the prevailing sentiment. A seven, of course, would wipe out the bets, but, when frozen, they are not affected by anything that happens on the roll.

PRESSING

To "press" a bet is to increase it by the same amount after it has won. Let's say you have a **place** bet on the six. A six is rolled. Instead of taking your entire winnings on the bet, you would press it by leaving on the amount of the winnings that was equal to the original bet—in short, doubling the bet.

As a general rule, it is foolish to press because you are depending on the number to repeat, and the odds against it are much too high. There **is** a time to press, though. It is when the roll is hot and you have **already made a profit** that is satisfactory to you. Then you can relax caution a bit.

What is satisfactory? I never press on a roll until I have my investment back plus an extremely large profit, generally double the investment. If I have invested, say, two hundred dollars in several bets, I start **thinking** about pressing when the betting has earned me four hundred dollars, and I won't actually begin pressing until my profit reaches five hundred dollars.

When I do start pressing, I begin with the safer bets, the numbers that come up frequently, such as six and eight. I do this even if I have collected a number of times on the six and eight and the five and nine, for instance, have not yet been rolled. Remember, it is easier to roll a six or an eight (because there are more ways to do it) than to roll a five or nine, so it is a mistake to assume that a shooter who has rolled three sixes or eights will be more likely to roll a five or nine before repeating the six or eight again. Each roll of the dice is a **new** roll, while probabilities are measured on eternity.

How long should you keep pressing? My policy is to leave the bets on until the shooter sevens out. Even though this means that I lose all the bets in the end I feel that it is worth it when the roll is hot. To pull off while a roll is still hot is to be overly cautious. I have seen too many excessively prudent players take their bets off and then watch in agony as the shooter continued to hit dozens of numbers. They theoretically saved a few hundred dollars, but in actuality missed thousands.

But, remember the first rule: Never press until after you have made the profit that satisfies you and are playing on the casino's money.

GOOD BETS AND BAD BETS

To repeat: the best a bettor can do is reduce the house's percentage to a minimum over a period of time.

Reducing the house's percentage, we now know, means making the bets on which the house has the least advantage. When I say "over a period of time," I mean making those bets when the dice are hot (if you are a right bettor), or cold (if you are a wrong bettor).

The dice will not be either hot or cold every time you step up to a table. Sometimes they will be so-so, winning part of the time, losing part of the time, having no clearly definable character. Don't be in a rush to get into the game. Wait for a period when the dice are either hot (if you are a right bettor) or cold (if you are a wrong bettor). Over a period of time, if you play only when the dice are on a streak and you make only those bets that reduce the house's advantage to a minimum, you will win.

You have to make up your mind, though, whether you are a right bettor or a wrong bettor, because the dice cannot be both hot and cold at the same time. And if you are playing when the dice are so-so and you try to guess whether they will go with the shooter or against the shooter on the next roll, you are ignoring the theory of probabilities. You are, in effect, treating craps as if it were the same as tossing a coin.

I am a right bettor. I bet when the dice are hot. For one reason: A hot table is an exciting table, with a great deal of action, while a cold table is slow, and—to me—boring.

That, however, is not the most important reason. My main motive is that right betting gives me the best edge I can possibly get. Although the percentage appears to be approximately the same on **pass** (right) and **don't pass** (wrong) bets, that is not exactly true. The reason rests with the odds. It is always best to be on the short end of a bet. That is, if the odds are two to one **against** something happening, it is preferable to bet that it **will** happen (as the right bettor does) and put up one dollar to win two dollars, than to bet that it will **not** happen (as the wrong bettor does) and put up two dollars to win one dollar. In the long run, a wrong bettor must invest more money than a right bettor to achieve the same result. And the run of bad dice for the wrong bettor must last longer than the run of good dice for the right bettor.

GOOD BETS

Pass Line

For the right bettor, the **pass** line bet with odds is the very best bet he can make. A **pass** line bettor wins, you will recall, when the shooter rolls a seven or eleven (natural) on the come-out, or rolls a point number (four, five, six, eight, nine or ten) on the come-out and then rolls that number again before rolling a seven (sevening out).

The percentage against the bettor on a straight **pass** line bet is 1.41. Taking the odds, the percentage is reduced to .84.

Conclusion: Play the **pass** line and take the odds. You can't do better.

Place Bet

When you make a **place** bet, you bet on a point number (four, five, six, eight, nine or ten). You bet that the shooter will roll your point number before he rolls a seven. With regard to odds, the four and ten, the five and nine, and the six and eight are paired. That is, the house odds are nine to five on the four and ten, seven to five on the five and nine, and seven to six on the six and eight. With these odds, the percentage against the bettor works out to 6.67 on four and ten, 4.0 on five and nine, and 1.51 on six and eight.

The advantage can be considerably reduced on four and ten by buying the number—paying a five-percent fee and getting the true odds, which on four and ten are two to one. Buying the number on five and nine and six and eight, however, has the reverse result, increasing rather than lowering the house's advantage.

Conclusion: After the **pass** line bet, the **place** bet is the next best—if you buy the four and ten and place the five and nine and six and eight. Using the **place** bets in this way, you get a maximum of action with a minimum of risk.

BAD BETS

Don't Pass Line

The bettor wins when the shooter rolls craps on the come-out (with either the two or twelve barred), or when the shooter rolls a point number on the come-out and then rolls a seven before repeating the point number.

Even with the two or twelve barred, the percentage against the **don't pass** bettor is only 1.40. If you give the odds the percentage is reduced to .83.

But, being a wrong bet, it requires an investment of more money and a longer run of bad dice than a right bet to achieve the same result. The elements of time (longer run) and investment (more money) make the **don't pass** bet considerably less effective for the player than the **pass** bet. This is especially true when the player is waiting for the table to get hot. While he is waiting, the factors of time and investment can wipe him out, with the result that when the table does get hot he no longer has money to play.

Conclusion: If it is in your blood to be a wrong bettor, play the **don't pass** line. But in comparison to the **pass** line, it is a bad bet.

Come Bet

The **come** bettor is a right bettor. When you put a bet on the **come** section you are betting on the next roll of the dice. If the shooter rolls a seven or eleven, you win. If the shooter rolls craps, you lose. If the shooter rolls a point number, your **come** bet is moved to the corresponding box number.

As long as the bet is in the **come** section, the percentage against you is the same as on a **pass** line bet. That's fine—the house's advantage is only 1.41. The hitch comes when the shooter rolls a point number and your bet is moved to that number on the **place** section. Now, in order for you to win, the shooter has to roll that number again.

When you make a **place** bet, you win when the number is rolled once. When you make a **come** bet, on the other hand, and your bet is moved to a number in the **place** section, the number has to be rolled twice before you can win—once to get it moved to the box number, then again after it is put into the **place** section.

In any series of rolls, probability dictates that there is less chance that a number will come up twice than that it will come up once. So, by making a **come** bet rather than a **place** bet, you are increasing the percentage against yourself.

Conclusion: A **come** bet is not the worst bet on the table, but, even so, it's on the wrong side of the line that separates the good bets from the bad bets.

Don't Come Bet

The **don't come** bettor is a wrong bettor. When you put a bet on the **don't come** section you are betting on the next roll of the dice. If the shooter rolls craps (barring the two or twelve) you win. If the shooter rolls a seven or eleven, you lose. If the shooter rolls a point number, your **don't come** bet is moved to the corresponding box number. As soon as the bet is moved, you win if the shooter sevens out, and lose if the shooter rolls his point number.

The deciding element in this case is that the **don't come** bet is a wrong bet. Consequently, as with the **don't pass** bet, it requires an investment of more money and a longer run of bad dice to achieve the same result that less money and a shorter run of good dice can produce with a right bet.

Conclusion: Don't bet the **don't come**.

Big 6 And Big 8

You are betting that the shooter will roll a six or an eight before he rolls a seven. But you would be better off making **place** bets. A **place** bet on the six or eight would pay off at odds of seven to six, while **Big 6 And Big 8** pays only even money. The house percentage on the **place** bet is 1.51, while the house advantage on the **Big 6 And Big 8** is 9.09 percent.

Conclusion: **Big 6 And Big 8** is a very bad bet. Don't be taken in.

Field Bet

A **field** bet is a one-roll bet. You win if any of the numbers two, three, four, nine, ten, eleven or twelve comes up. You collect double on the two or twelve. If any other number—five, six, seven or eight—comes up, you lose.

The fact that you have seven numbers going for

you on a **field** bet and only four going against you makes it look attractive. But it is all illusion. Because the four numbers that are against you can be made in twenty ways, while the seven numbers in your favor can be made only sixteen ways. The possibility of collecting double on the two or twelve reduces the probability rate a bit, but not enough. The percentage is still 2.56 in the casino's favor.

Conclusion: In craps, as in love, if you play the **field** it will undoubtedly cost you. Don't play the **field.**

Hardways

When you make a **hardways** bet you are betting that certain combinations of numbers will come up. The combinations are: two and two to make a four; three and three to make a six; four and four to make an eight; and five and five to make a ten. You lose if a seven is thrown before the combination comes up or if the number is made by some other combination (for instance, if ten is made with a six and four).

The actual odds against making a four or a ten the hard way are eight to one. The house pays seven to one, giving the house an advantage of 11.1 percent. The true odds against making a six or an eight the hard way are ten to one, and the house pays off at nine to one, giving the casino an edge of 9.0 percent.

Conclusion: The casino's advantage is far too large. Pass up the **hardways.**

Any Seven

A one-roll bet. You are betting that on the next roll of the dice a seven will come up, making you a winner. If any other number is rolled, you're a loser.

The house pays four to one on an **any seven** bet. The casino's percentage is a whopping 16.7.

Conclusion: The worst bet on the table. A sucker bet.

Any Craps

Another one-roll bet. You bet that a two, three or twelve (normally, craps) will come up on the next throw.

The odds against any of these numbers being thrown on one roll are eight to one. The house pays off at seven to one, thus the advantage for the casino is 11.1 percent.

Conclusion: An atrocious bet. Pretend it isn't even there.[1]

Propositions

This is a one-roll bet on which you wager that a certain number will be thrown on the next toss of the dice. The numbers that can be bet are two, three, eleven and twelve, or, in the **hop** bet, any other specified combination of two numbers.

[1] Note: Players sometimes employ **any seven** bets and **any craps** bets as "insurance" bets. The theory is that a right bettor can insure himself against getting wiped out if the shooter rolls craps on the come-out (he would lose on the **pass** line bet, but win on the **any craps** bet). Similarly, a right bettor can supposedly insure himself, at least on one roll, against losing entirely if the shooter, rolling for a point, sevens out (he will lose on the **pass** line bet, but win on the **any seven** bet). The fallacy is that the cost of the insurance is too high. The percentage against the bettor remains at 11.1 on **any craps** and 16.7 on **any seven**. And a bad bet by any other name, in this case "insurance," is still a bad bet.

The odds against a two or a twelve coming up are thirty-five to one. The house pays thirty for one, giving itself an advantage of 13.89 percent. The odds against a three or an eleven or other specified combination being rolled are seventeen to one. The house pays fifteen for one and gets an 11.1 percent advantage.[2]

Conclusion: Don't let the house proposition you. Play no **proposition** bets.

Turn Bet, Horn Bet, Eleven Bet

I described these in Chapter 3. They are too ridiculous to deserve any more space or comment. The only logical reason for making these bets is an insane desire to get rid of your money. Flush it down the drain instead. It will save you a walk to the crap tables and achieve the same result.

Finally, for quick reference, the table on page 88 shows how the casino pays off on the various bets and the resulting percentage in favor of the house.

---

[2] Another note: The odds I have given on the bets in the "square"—**any seven, any craps,** and so on, are the real odds you get as opposed to the odds you might think you are getting. On the layout, you will notice, the wording on the seven bet is "5 for 1." That is not the same as "5 to 1." When you bet a dollar, say, at five **for** one and win, you get back the dollar you bet plus four dollars. So, five **for** one actually amounts to four **to** one. If you had received odds of five **to** one and won, you would have received the dollar you bet plus five dollars. The same applies to the other bets in the square. Ten for one is really nine to one; fifteen for one is actually fourteen to one, and so on. The casino is not above using semantics to its own advantage.

Bet	Payoff	P.C.
pass	even money	1.41
don't pass	even money	1.40
come	even money	1.41
don't come	even money	1.40
pass + odds	even + odds	.84
don't pass + odds	even + odds	.83
field	even money	2.56
4 or 10 place	nine to five	6.67
5 or 9 place	seven to five	4.0
6 or 8 place	seven to six	1.51
big 6 and big 8	even money	9.09
any craps	seven to one	11.1
hardway 4 or 10	seven to one	11.1
hardway 6 or 8	nine to one	9.09
11 or 3 proposition	fourteen to one	11.1
12 or 2 proposition	twenty-nine to one	13.9
any seven	four to one	16.7

HOW YOU SAY IT

It isn't absolutely necessary to know the jargon of the game. The dealer won't refuse to pay you your winnings if you roll a seven on the come-out and fail to call it a natural, nor will he decline to take your money if you throw snake eyes on the come-out and refer to it as "two ones." But it will probably contribute to your enjoyment of the game if you know the tongue. So, with that purpose in mind, here is a glossary of the terms that, if learned, will enable you to speak the language.

ACE: The one-spot on a die.
ACEY-DEUCEY: A combination of the one-spot on one die and the two-spot on the other die.
ACTION: The betting.

BACK BET: An odds bet on the **pass** line.

BACKBOARD: The raised edge around the crap table against which the dice should be thrown.

BANK: The house.

BANKER: A dealer.

BAR: To withhold a number from paying off.

BIG DICK: The point ten.

BOXCARS: A roll of two sixes.

BOXMAN: The houseman who handles the money and is in charge of the game.

COLD: A cold table; a table that is losing for the right bettors.

COME-OUT: The initial roll of the dice.

CRAPS: Rolling a two, a three or a twelve.

DEALER: The houseman who collects and pays off bets for the house.

DIE: A six-sided plastic cube, with dots representing the numbers one through six.

EDGE: An advantage.

EIGHTER FROM DECATUR: The point eight.

HOT: A hot table; a table that is winning for the right bettors.

HOUSE: The operator of a gambling game, the casino.

LAYOUT: The diagram imprinted on the crap table, with sections for different bets.

LIMIT: The maximum amount that can be wagered on any one bet.

LITTLE JOE: The point four.

MARKER: An IOU.

NATURAL: A seven or eleven thrown on the come-out roll.

NO DICE: A roll that does not count.

ODDS: The ratio of unfavorable probabilities to favorable probabilities.

ONE-ROLL BET: A bet that is decided on the next roll of the dice.

PERCENTAGE: The house advantage, obtained by paying off at less than the true odds.

PHOEBE: The point five.

POINT: Any of the numbers four, five, six, eight, nine or ten which the shooter rolls on the come-out and then tries to repeat before throwing a seven.

RACK: The groove in the raised edge around the table where the chips rest when not in use.

ROLL: To throw the dice.

SHAVE: To alter the dimensions of the dice and upset their balance, causing certain numbers to come up more or less often than the odds dictate.

SHOOTER: The player who rolls the dice.

SNAKE EYES: A combination of two one-spots on the dice.

STICKMAN: The houseman in charge of the dice.

VIGORISH: A fee paid to the house in order to get the true odds on a bet as opposed to the house odds.

BEYOND BETTING- THE EDGE

So far, I have not revealed any information that is not available to anyone who might want to learn it. I don't think there is anyone who plays craps but doesn't know that the odds on the bets are in favor of the house. Not all players know the exact percentages or realize how much the percentages vary from bet to bet, but if they are ignorant of the facts it isn't because the facts are being withheld from them. There is no conspiracy by the casinos to keep the players ignorant.

The fault lies with the bettors. They don't make the effort to find out the facts. They prefer to believe that they can overcome the casinos' advantage with luck, a superstition or a system. Even if they knew the percentages and used that knowledge—betting as I have suggested—they still would not be certain to win. For there is more to it than simply knowing what bets to make.

So, let's now consider the additional factors: the elements that give the player the edge he needs to win.

THE RIGHT TABLE

To win, as I mentioned before, it is necessary to concentrate your betting on a period when the dice are on a streak—a hot streak if you are a right bettor, a cold streak if you are a wrong bettor. Otherwise the advantage you gain by knowing how to bet will be dissipated by the time element. For example if you are a right bettor and you play for any length of time at a cold table, waiting for it to get hot, by the time the table changes—if it does—you will probably be so far behind that it will be impossible even to catch up, let alone get ahead.

When you arrive at the casino, don't immediately set up in business at the first table in sight. Play it cool. Suppress that urge to get into action. The tables won't go away; they will be there long after you have gone. Move about, going from table to table, keeping your eyes and ears open and your wallet closed. Bide your time—you cobra—and strike when the prey is vulnerable.

It isn't likely that you will find a hot table right away. If you do, move in and begin playing. What you will be looking for, though—and will be more apt to find—is a promising table, a warm table. Tables, in a way, are like societies; they change more by evolution than by revolution. By that I mean that it is more probable that a warm table will **gradually** get hot than that a cold table will **suddenly** get hot. Where big money is involved, evidently, the dominating philosophy always tends to be conservative.

How to spot a promising table: First, look at the players' faces. Are they happy faces? If they are, the play, in a moderate way, is in favor of the bettors (at a hot table, the expressions are ecstatic). Don't mistake smiles of anticipation, however, for genuine happiness. Such smiles, examined closely, have a forced look. The players aren't truly happy; they are merely biting the bullet. A smile of anticipation is not in the strict sense a bona fide smile. It is a tentative facial expression that is more often than not about to become a wince.

If wrong bettors reacted to winning in the same fashion as right bettors, a cold table could be spotted by looking for one or two delighted faces (since wrong bettors are always the minority at the tables). But it doesn't work that way. Wrong bettors learned their expression at the poker table. They are all members of a secret society, the first and only commandment of which is: Thou shalt not in any way show any emotion. The penalty for breaking that commandment is a week of making expressive faces in front of a mirror.

There is a good reason for the wrong bettors' determination to imitate a zero. The majority of the other players at the table are optimistic; they are expecting the dice to win and they are backing that expectation with cash. The wrong bettor, on the other hand, is hoping that the dice will lose and—the right bettors fully realize—is focusing all of his occult power (luck) on bringing about that negative result.

Understandably, the many right bettors view the wrong bettors as The Enemy. The conflict, as far as I know, has not yet degenerated into actual violence. But for the wrong bettor the threat of it is there. It is not outside the reach of possibility that someday a band of right bettors, provoked beyond endurance by a wrong bettor's killing at a dice table, will form into a lynch party. Consequently, wrong bettors try their best to go unnoticed. Their secret society, I understand, is supporting research aimed at developing a method for making them invisible.

Anyway, on your hunt for a promising table, look for a preponderance of genuinely happy faces. But don't stop at that. You may be a poor judge of what is a genuinely happy face. So look also for other indicators. Remember, your objective is to win, despite the heavy odds against it, and you can't accomplish that purpose if you go about it in a slipshod way.

A survey of the amount of chips at the table and the manner in which they are handled will help. If the chips are plentiful in the rack (the groove around the edge of the table), it is a sign that the bettors are at least breaking even—a warm table. But if the rack is getting bare it is an indication that a lot of losing is going on. Above all, stay away from a table where the bettors are holding their chips in their hands. That means they don't have many chips left. Those players have already lost most of their stake and are in the throes of the death rattle that precedes rigor mortis—a frigid table.

You might also look for bulging pockets. Some players, for a reason known only to themselves, do not want other players to know that they are winning, so, instead of keeping their chips in the rack, they will stuff them into their jacket pockets. This is called "sink money," for the reason that the players are sinking it away, I assume. Anyway, bulging pockets are comparable to full racks.

The ideal table, of course, is the one where both racks and pockets are full—where winnings have spilled over from racks to pockets. And make sure that the majority of the racks and/or pockets are filled. Don't make the mistake of thinking that you have hit a hot table when, in fact, you have only found a table where three or four friends have just walked over together and taken money on markers from the house.

The simplest way to determine how a table is going, of course, is to ask one of the players. The answer cannot always be depended upon, however. Some players want to keep a good table a secret (on the theory, possibly, that any change, such as a new player, will disturb the good "vibrations"). Such players' replies to a direct question will usually be evasive.

Never, for Pete's sake, join a game that is just starting. How can you possibly tell whether a table is hot or cold before the game even gets rolling? More importantly, though, it may be a come-on. Occasionally, when business is slow, the casino manager will send some of his employees (not boxmen, stickmen, dealers or pitmen, who are forbidden by local laws to play where they're employed) out into the void to stir up some action. They will start a game, pretending to be customers, but they are simply shills.

A game like this has no chance of ever heating up. Real customers have a capacity for working up honest-to-God enthusiasm at a crap table. But house employees, living with gambling day in and day out, develop a blasé attitude toward it. Pretending to be customers doesn't change them. Their presence at a table as make-believe customers—even if they wear false noses and fake beards—can put a freeze on the table that will linger for days. That is a scientific fact.

Don't be drawn into a game by a high roller—a player who throws his money around as if hundred-dollar bills came as premiums in cereal boxes. A high roller bets big with total abandon. He creates a great deal of excitement at a table. The other players encourage him—and loudly (what the hell, it isn't **their** money). The excitement is, as romantic novelists used to write, at fever pitch.

But betting big does not necessarily result in winning big. Over any length of time, betting with abandon can only make a player a loser. In a case where a high roller is at work, the noise at the table is no guarantee that the table is hot. It could have icicles hanging on it for all most high rollers know.

I assume that a high roller's goal is not to win but to draw attention to himself, mistaking attention for respect. If that is it, he is wasting not only his money but also his time and energy. When he is finished and exits, the other players' attention quickly reverts to themselves. And if he is looking for respect from the professionals he will have sevened out on that too. Their respect goes to the "tough" player, who may bet high but never wildly.

So, ten seconds of compassion for the high rollers of the world. The poor bastards have already paid for it in one way or another.

CONTROL

The paragraphs in this section are probably the most important in the book. They have to do with self-control. If, as a craps player, you can't establish a set of intelligent rules for yourself and follow and stick to it, then, as sure as a worm has two ends, you will lose. If you are not willing or able to ignore the temptations and distractions that your own human nature and the casino will hassle you with, then you might as well stop reading this book right now. Nothing I have written so far or will advise hereafter will be able to make you a winner.

A Limit

The house has a limit. It puts a ceiling on the amount of money a player can wager on any one bet, and it isn't often that it lifts that restriction. It sets the limit to protect itself, to make sure that the casino will not suffer unduly on those occasions when the dice get hot for certain players and they are making winning roll after winning roll.

What is an astute business practice for the house is an astute business practice for the bettor. Set a limit for yourself. Not on how much money you will wager on each bet (we'll cover that aspect shortly), but on how much you will lose before you face the fact that, baby, it just is not your night, and quit.

Setting a limit, of course, is simple. So is stopping smoking—until you want a cigarette. The crunch comes when you reach your limit and then have a hunch—or are communicated with by some other means of divine intervention—that you are ripe to begin winning. One more bet can't hurt, can it? Yes, sir, it can. It can lead to one more additional "get even" bet, then another and another. Before you know it, you're smoking two packs a day again.

Don't try to kid yourself that you are sticking to your limit when you know you are not. Once, in Las Vegas, when a friend complained to me that he had lost $4,000 at the crap tables the night before, I suggested to him that in order to avoid that kind of tragedy in the future he ought to set a limit for himself. He told me that he already had a limit —five hundred dollars. Having a rudimentary knowledge of figures, I found it hard to understand how, with a limit of five hundred dollars, he could possibly lose $4,000. As it turned out, he had spent the previous night going from casino to casino, betting his "limit" at each place. I didn't try to explain to him that he didn't actually have a limit. He knew that, but just didn't want to recognize it. He preferred to pride himself on his self-control.

Put yourself on a strict regimen. If you are going to Las Vegas or Puerto Rico or wherever for three days, say, and you have fifteen hundred dollars that you can afford to lose at the crap tables, budget it over the three-day period at five hundred dollars a night. But, most importantly, **stick to the schedule.**

If you lose the first five hundred dollars the first night, don't borrow from the second night—not even if you hear "voices" whispering to you that one more roll of the dice will change your luck. Instead, go have a good dinner and watch the show in the main room. For the time being, your betting money is gone. Be happy that you didn't stay at the tables and dig yourself into a $1,000 or $1,500 hole in one night. You'll find that you won't hear the "voices" anymore—**nothing** can be heard over the din in the main room.

Concentration

A cold table is usually so quiet that you can hear the inaudible sounds of well-laid plans gone wrong. But hot tables are invariably busy and noisy. The shooter is exhorting the dice to continue their winning ways. The right bettors are shouting encouragement and advice to the shooter. Attractive young ladies are hawking cigarettes and drinks. And nonplayers are crowding around, making even more noise than the players.

To win, you must somehow shut out these distractions and keep your attention focused unblinkingly on the game. That is not to say that you can't join in creating the cacophony. Half the fun of playing craps is contributing to the general exultation when a table gets hot. On such occasions, I probably make more noise than anyone else at the table. But at the same time I keep my mind on the play. I exhort, I shout—**but I don't listen.**

Not listening to yourself is easier than it might seem. Consider this: When you and your neighbor meet in the morning when you are both taking out the garbage and your neighbor asks you how things are going and you reply that things are fine, do you **think** about the exchange? I doubt it. Your neighbor isn't really asking how things are and you aren't really telling him. The two of you are merely acknowledging each other's existence.

The same applies to the things said at the crap tables. They are chants. When you plead with the dice to roll numbers, it isn't necessary to think about it, or even to listen to your own words. In fact, I suspect, if you **do** take it seriously enough to pay attention to it, you probably shouldn't be at the crap table; you are playing not with your mind but with your emotions. And, believe me, those dice are not for one minute fooled into thinking that they **must** roll numbers.

Don't drink when you're at the crap table, even though the drinks are free to players and are handed out by beautiful young women. The drinks won't really be free. They will affect your judgment, and in the end will cost you dearly. If you drink, save the drinking until you leave the table. Then, if your judgment is impaired, it is less likely to cost you money.

The distraction that is most difficult to ignore is the nonplayer who stands at your elbow and hands out advice. The advice is all bad. So bad, usually, that not even the compulsive suckers are tempted to take it. The problem is that these nonplaying seers are cornucopias, dispensing nonsense in a never-ending flow. And the babble, if you let it, can drive you to thinking favorably about strangulation as a legitimate means of dealing with boors.

I once tried to get rid of a self-appointed counselor by turning away from the table, giving him my full attention, and explaining to him that I couldn't accept his advice because I was a member of a cult whose members made their betting decisions by examining the entrails of barn swallows. It didn't do any good. He was fascinated by the notion—thought it had a lot going for it—and wanted to hear about it in detail. If I'd had a membership application for the cult, I could have signed him up on the spot.

Since then I have reached the conclusion that,

like high rollers and people who make obscene phone calls, it is attention and attention only that the nonplaying advice-givers want. I now respond by not responding. When they sidle up to me and begin the babble, I tune them out, ignoring them completely, not even recognizing their existence. I sometimes have pangs about it; I don't get any pleasure out of cutting people dead. But I've found that it's the only defense that works.

A few seconds of compassion for advice-givers, too—but not as much as for high rollers and obscene phone callers.

Betting, Winning and Losing

Know what bets you are going to make before you go to the table. If you intend to do what I do, that means making **pass** line bets, taking odds, buying the four and ten, and **placing** the other point numbers. Having decided on a plan, don't—no matter what—detour from it. Be a rock.

When the table gets hot and it appears that all you have to do to win is make a bet, it is easy to be influenced by the euphoric atmosphere and become greedy. At that point, the sucker bets—the **field, any seven, any craps,** and so on—begin to look good to you. At the same time, the stickman will be encouraging you in this delusion, calling out, "Bet the **field!**" You know in your mind that not even a blessing by the house chaplain could make these bets good bets. But contradicting this truth is the unmistakable evidence that you have suddenly become invincible, that you can't lose no matter how foolishly you bet.

Well, that's what Hitler thought when he sidetracked twenty-two divisions from the war in the West and sent them east to overrun Stalingrad and conquer Russia. The Russian winter and the Russian Army did to Hitler's invincibility what they had done, decades earlier, to Napoleon's. And that is what deviating from your plan and scattering your bets all over the table will do for your chance to emerge from the game a winner—cool it off and put it to rout.

When the table is hot and you are winning consistently, yes, bet more money. But not on different bets. Rather, increase the amount on the bets you are already making—**the bets that reduce the casino's advantage to the minimum.** That way, you are increasing the advantage you gained when the table got hot. The other way, you are frittering it away.

To be able to increase your bets appreciably you have to start out betting moderately—you can't begin by betting the house limit and then increase it later. Betting moderately is the way you **should** bet at the beginning, when the table is not yet hot. Otherwise you are liable to piddle away your stake before the table ever heats up. I won't try to define "moderate" in terms of dollars. It depends on your own circumstance. One man's pocket money is another man's fortune.

What do I mean, then, by moderate betting? It is testing the water, getting into the game, so to speak, one foot at a time instead of diving in. When making **place** bets, for instance, I begin by betting two numbers, usually the six and eight because they're the numbers, aside from the seven, which come up most often. Then, after I feel comfortable at the table, I lengthen my range to three numbers, adding bets on the five or nine. I begin placing all of the numbers **only** after I'm winning consistently.

That is the practical application of my particular definition of moderate betting. You can vary it.

But the essential point is: Do not leap in. Risk only a minor portion of your stake at the beginning, and save the major portion for the hot roll. Because the more money you have to bet when the hot roll comes, the more money you will win.

At a promising table the winnings will generally fluctuate between the right bettors and the wrong bettors (with the house, understand, winning always, collecting from the wrong bettors when the right bettors win and vice versa). There is a temptation, consequently, to try to go with the shifts, to vary your wagering between right betting and wrong betting. Don't do it. It is another example of trying to reduce to a guessing game a process that is controlled by the laws of probabilities. More often than not when you "gee" the dice will "haw."

Now, the table is hot. You are sticking to your plan and winning. Then, suddenly, right in the middle of a hallucination in which you see yourself winning big enough to buy a country of your own and run it the way a country ought to be run, the roll goes stone cold—the shooter sevens out. What do you do? First, naturally, you make a mental note to kick your dog when you get home. But after that, what?

The instant the shooter sevens out, you thank your lucky stars that you came out of the experience as well as you did—**and you quit!** You don't stay at the table, hoping that the next roll will be just as hot as the last. That might happen. But the chances are that it won't. And don't begin doubling your bets, thinking that by increasing the action you can somehow stimulate the table to rev up its motor again, the way a human heart will sometimes react to massaging. Doubling your bets will only cause you to lose double.

Be content. Tip the housemen, then take your winnings and get out of the game room. If, passing the slot machines, you inadvertently happen to knock over a few little old ladies, don't even stop to apologize. Because **winning depends on quitting when you are ahead.** Casino owners buy their own countries on the money they take from bettors who aren't satisfied with just winning, but want to win it all.

About tipping: Every once in a while during the game and especially when the betting is heavy, the stickman will suggest that a player "make a bet for the boys." The boys are those muscular, machine-made house employees at the table—dealers, stickmen and boxmen—who are anything but boys. The suggestion is that a bet be made, with the winnings to go to the boys. In other words, a tip that they will share.

My own rules on tipping are: I never make a bet for the boys, and when I am asked to do so, I do not tip at all. Because when I am asked to make a bet for the boys, I am being hustled, and I have an aversion to being hustled. Most of the time, though, I do tip—but only after I have finished playing. Then, if I have won big, I tip big, giving the table personnel chips, which can be converted to cash. If I have lost, I do not tip—for the simple reason that I don't ask them to tip me when I lose.

In general, I am in favor of tipping, but not for sentimental reasons. There's a practical reason: The boys remember. And when a table gets hot and gets crowded, they are more likely to make room for a tipper than for a nontipper.

The Trials of Winning

You're a winner! You've cashed in your chips and your pockets are bulging with greenbacks. But, what to do with it?

Don't hang on to it—not all of it. Don't try to carry it around with you—all of the muggers are not in New York City all of the time. They go to the casinos too. Don't keep it in your hotel room—second-story men, these days, are twentieth-story men and they work the high-rise hotels. And, while you still have it all, don't go anywhere near a crap table.

I was taught how to play craps by a friend, an entertainer who at that time was being paid $10,000 a week at a Las Vegas hotel. When he received his check each week, he kept sixty dollars of the ten thousand to gamble with and sent the rest to his bank for deposit. It is a wise example to follow.

When you win, first subtract the amount of your original stake. If you started, for instance, with five hundred dollars and after winning you have $1,500, put aside five hundred dollars. The difference, one thousand dollars, is your winnings. Convert the winnings into some form other than cash —a check from the casino, a traveler's check—and mail it to yourself at your home or office. That way it won't be within easy grasp, considerably lessening the chances that the casino will get it back from you before you leave.

Another way to protect yourself from yourself—a method that has a particularly attractive advantage—is to get your winnings in the form of a marker (IOU) from the casino. This service is not available to everyone, but if you are a fairly regular customer the courtesy will probably be extended. A marker, in this case, is a slip of paper that says that the casino owes you a certain amount of money. You will receive the marker and the casino will retain a copy. When you return home, you contact the casino's representative in your city. He will have the casino's copy of the marker. Your marker will be exchanged—for cash, not a check. Then both the marker and the casino's copy of it will be ceremonially burned.

The advantage is that now there is no record of your winning. So, whether you report the money to the Internal Revenue Service is entirely up to you and your conscience. I understand that some players do not report their winnings. I am told, in fact, that this dodge is quite popular with winning craps players. And, this being a world full of human beings, I can't say that I doubt the claim in the least. I am not recommending the method, however—only reporting on a story that it is used quite freely.

After you get your winnings safely out of reach —whatever means you use to do it—you are ready to begin again, if you desire. You still have your stake, and you know your limit, and the tables are waiting.

So, roll 'em!

Attitude

As with most ventures, the way you approach craps playing is important to the outcome. In sport, the player who convinces himself that he can win has a better chance of doing it than the player who is less certain. Unfortunately, this "can do" attitude does not apply to craps. All the self-confidence in the world won't make the dice do what you want them to do.

Your attitude should not be toward the dice, but toward the casino. I look at the casino as a competitor. We are involved in a business transaction. The casino, at the start, has the best of it. But if I follow the rules I have laid down in this book, I can overcome that advantage and win. It's that simple—or that complex.

I'm not suggesting that you be belligerent about it. Belligerence, in fact, is a handicap. It leads to thinking of the casino not simply as a business competitor but as an enemy. Enemies must be killed—symbolically, if not actually. To kill the casino, you have to win all its money, leave it destitute—for money, of course, is its life blood. Trying to do that tempts you to excesses, blinds you to the reality of the theory of probabilities. In the end, you fall on your own sword.

So, relax. Enjoy. Play the game intelligently. Resist the urge to go for blood. Don't spend all your time at the crap tables. See the shows. Eat the food. Go out every once in a while and look up at the sky—it won't hurt your luck. Don't make a compulsion of craps even for a short period of time.

After all—it's only a game.

THE FORMULA

When a congressman learned from an aide that he had been booked at a dinner to speak for a half hour on the subject "Integrity in Politics," he protested that telling all he knew on the subject would take him at the most ten minutes. As a solution to filling the time, the aide suggested that he "tell them what you're going to tell them, then tell them, then tell them what you've told them."

I am now going to tell you what I told you. Not to stretch the speech, but to sum up in a brief way all that I have advised that bears directly on playing craps and winning, so that any aspect of the formula can be referred to quickly.

If you should find yourself at a crap table and in dire need of refreshing your memory on some point that has been covered here, it would not be prudent to ask the boxman to hold up the game while you page through the entire book. This way, it will be necessary to refer only to a single chapter.

What follows, then, is The Formula—my method of playing craps, from the moment I enter the casino until I leave, a winner.

THE RIGHT TABLE

When you arrive at the casino, your objective will be to find a hot table. There probably won't be one at the moment, so settle for a warm table and bide your time, betting moderately. A warm table is recognizable mainly by the genuinely happy faces of the players and the full racks of chips.

At a cold table the majority of the players are in mourning and holding the few chips they have left in their hands, getting ready to depart for the bar, where they will blame their disaster on bad luck.

Never start a table. It may be a come-on. Certainly, it cannot establish its character until betting has been in progress for a length of time.

SUPERSTITIONS AND SYSTEMS

A bettor who relies on a superstition is depending on blind faith to overcome the reality of probabilities; patently ridiculous if you **think** about it. If a rabbit's foot could control the roll of the dice, the rabbits, having four, would have wiped out the casinos long ago.

Systems are no better. A formula is not necessarily valid simply because it is based on mathematics. The people who invent the systems don't use them; they peddle them to the gullible.

BETTING

Play the **pass** line and take the odds, and buy the four and ten and make **place** bets on the other point numbers, six and eight and five and nine.

Until the table gets hot, bet moderately. When the table heats up, increase your action—but do it by increasing the amount of your bets, not by pressing.

Do not, under any circumstances, make sucker bets. These include **Big 6 And Big 8**, the **field, hardways, any seven, any craps** and **proposition** bets.

LIMIT

Your limit is how much you can afford to lose. That is not the same as how much you can afford to lose if you get a second mortgage on your house, borrow on your car and put your wife and children up for sale. When you lose your limit, quit—period. After you have saved up enough to have a limit again, go back to the casino and try once more—but not before. Winning depends on knowing when to quit.

CONCENTRATION

A hot table is a noisy table. Tune out all noise that you yourself are not making and pay no attention to your own.

Don't drink when you are at the crap table—not even if you are sure that you can handle it and, as proof, can cite the fact that your wife agrees with you. Why do anything that can adversely affect your judgment? One scotch and soda can sometimes make an **any seven** bet look like the magic formula.

Don't get drawn into conversations with non-players when you are at the table. A "hello" is the most they are entitled to hear from you. After that, if they continue to advise you on how to shoot or how to bet, taking your attention from the game, give them the cold shoulder.

HOT ROLL

Don't get the idea that one hot roll will be followed by another hot roll. Sometimes it happens, but not very often. When the hot roll ends, don't try to persuade yourself that if you stay at the table a little while longer it will come back. When they go, they go bag and baggage. Face the fact that the romance is over and leave the table. There will always be another new romance another day or an hour later.

GREED

Don't take greed to the dice table with you. It will only tempt you to play wildly, making sucker bets and staying too long at the table. Save greed for the really important things—sex and licorice jelly beans.

TIPPING

In general, tip. The "boys" at the tables remember, and yesterday's tip may get you playing space at today's hot and crowded table.

Don't tip, however, by making a bet for the boys. Tip when you are finished playing.

When you win big, tip big. When you lose, don't tip at all. Share the adversity as well as the good fortune.

WINNINGS

The money you have when you leave the table that you didn't have when you arrived is your profit—your winnings. Get it out of reach fast! Convert it into something other than cash—a casino check, a traveler's check—and mail it to yourself at your home or office. If you can't get your hands on it, the casino can't get it back from you.

ATTITUDE

Craps is not a game. It is a business, with you and the casino as competitors. Your goal is to come out of it with a profit—which you **can** do—not to drive your competitor into bankruptcy—which you **can't** do. Treat the game as a business venture, in which you win a few, lose a few, but, if you are an astute businessman, you will win more than you lose.

Above all: Enjoy.

THE JOINTS

The following is a list of places around the world where you can find first-class gambling action. But please understand that, in preparing this list, I am neither (a) striving for completeness nor (b) claiming that all the information which appears below is absolutely accurate nor (c) even indulging in the forlorn hope that accurate information will still be accurate by the time this book gets through the publishing and printing processes and into your hands.

As far as completeness is concerned, this just isn't possible, or, for that matter, desirable. In a town like Las Vegas, where gambling is the principal industry, and where you can get action of a sort (meaning slot machines) the moment you get off your plane and into the airport building, there are a million little restaurants, bars and similar places of business which offer a gambling table or two along with all their other treats. The same is true, to a lesser extent, throughout England, where gambling isn't the principal industry, of course, but nevertheless a reasonably flourishing one. But the trouble with the tenth-rate places is that, at best, they're often so sparsely attended that you can find yourself in a dull and boring game in which you're the only participant, playing all alone against a combined stickman–pit boss–proprietor; or, at worst, playing with dice to which the proprietor has added several interesting weights which are not designed to make you richer. Obviously, I can't recommend these places and won't list them. I'm also not going to list any of the rather well-known but illegal gambling emporiums located in certain garden spots in New Jersey, Kentucky, Ohio, California, and other states. I don't patronize these places because I feel that it's impossible to concentrate properly on the game when you're conscious all the time of the mobster-guards scattered all around the place, sitting on high perches with grease guns (that means machine guns, neighbor) nestled in their arms; or when you're constantly looking over your shoulder in fear that the joint will be busted because somebody forgot to pay off the local constabulary that week. So I give my business strictly to legal establishments, and I think you should, too.

And as far as accuracy is concerned, in lists of this sort, that isn't possible, either. At some of the smaller places, particularly those outside the United States, the financing is so precarious that all it takes to put a joint out of business is for a group of big-time players to show up one weekend and hit them hard. On the other hand, some of the bigger places are so prosperous that a hotel which may have had one thousand rooms yesterday may start adding a wing today and have fifteen hundred rooms by the time this reaches you. There are also places which vacillate as their fortunes vary, oozing with hospitality when patrons have been unfortunate and switching abruptly to tightfistedness when players begin to walk away from the tables with bulging pockets.

The best bet, then, would be to regard this list as a reasonably accurate picture of the way things were the last time I looked—which wasn't necessarily yesterday or even the day before yesterday in some places. And just make sure you double-check with a long-distance or overseas phone call or two before setting out to visit a particular place or establishment. The joint may have turned into a garage by the time you call, particularly if some friends and I happened to visit it the week before. (That isn't boasting, really. It's praying.)

1. THE UNITED STATES

Las Vegas, Nevada

• ALADDIN. A small place on the Strip, legitimate enough but not really big time. Good for a modest, quiet game if you're in that sort of mood.

• CAESAR'S PALACE. A relatively new and extremely lavish hotel, and a good place to gamble because you can find a lot of hot tables going there all around the clock. Good food and good shows; as this is written, the stars who have just appeared there or will open in the near future include Frank Sinatra, Petula Clark, Paul Anka, and Diana Ross.

• CIRCUS CIRCUS. Another rather new place on the Strip which features circus acts (the Ringling Brothers kind, not the X-rated) going on all around you on tiers while you play. Amusing and entertaining place for a look and a drink, but distracting if you're serious about your game.

• DESERT INN. First class, but one of the quieter places on the Strip, and therefore popular with the golf and family crowds. Excellent food and good-looking surroundings. Until recently, their shows were mostly vaudeville-type revues of the wholesome variety, but they've begun to return to star appearances. Typical of the people currently booked there are Juliet Prowse, Bobbie Gentry, Jack Carter and Debbie Reynolds.

• DUNES. This is my favorite joint in Las Vegas, mostly because the junkets and the hospitality are handled by a man named Julie Weintraub. Julie is called "Big Julie" because he's about seven feet tall and equally wide. He has craggy features and looks tough, but, like many big men, he's really both a gentle man and a gentleman. The **Dunes** was bottom-of-the-barrel once upon a time, but the story, possibly apocryphal, is that Julie was a businessman who lost too much money at the tables and paid off by hiring himself to the hotel as a sort of entrepreneur who brought in plane-loads of businessmen-friends to gamble, thereby inventing the junket. Whether the story is totally true, partially true, or not at all true, Julie has long since become a full-time employee of the hotel (and perhaps even a part-owner), and the hotel has become huge and, in my opinion, remains the best in town. Excellent food and accommodations, friendly staff, good games.

• FOUR QUEENS. A big, wildly active in-town casino. Totally legit and okay, but, as I said earlier,

I don't really recommend the town joints except for a look.

• FREMONT. An in-town hotel, and sort of seedy. Their current show is a not-especially-updated version of Minsky's Burlesque, which should tell you something. The showroom is often half empty, and so, I'm afraid, is the casino.

• FRONTIER. A hotel and casino on the Strip which has had as many lives as a cat; it's been called the **Frontier** and the **New Frontier,** and is now called the **Frontier** again. It's currently trying very hard with name performers like Robert Goulet, Carol Lawrence and Phil Harris, and I'm told by friends who stayed there recently that it's no **Caesar's Palace** or **Dunes** but not too bad.

• HILTON FLAMINGO. Oldest hotel still in existence on the Strip, but it's well-maintained and still very good. Stars currently booked include people like Sandler and Young, Marty Allen, and Leslie Uggams.

• LANDMARK. This is another relatively new place in the Strip area, and it's struggling. It ran into difficulties, financial or managerial, while under construction, and stayed partially built for a long time. And it hasn't been knocking the town dead since it opened. The **Landmark** is a long, thin edifice with the main gambling room at the top level, reached by elevator. The last time I went up there, the games, show and food were all so-so, but it may get better.

• LAS VEGAS HILTON. Rather new and extremely big time. This hotel opened with a smash, luring Barbra Streisand back to Las Vegas by paying her an astronomical salary (reportedly the biggest ever paid in the town), and it's been swinging ever since. Stars currently scheduled to open there include Elvis Presley, Bill Cosby, Glen Campbell, and Tony Bennett. A lot of good restaurants and plenty of active tables.

• MGM GRAND HOTEL. Metro-Goldwyn-Mayer's entry into the gambling world, and the newest of the Strip hotels. As big as a city, with everything from a wide variety of restaurants to jai alai games. As this is written, the place is operating but still not completely finished, so patrons get the chattering of trip-hammers along with their gaming. It's obviously, however, going to be one of **the** in-places. Dean Martin, Shecky Greene, and Barbara Eden are among the performers booked.

• THE MINT. A gigantic downtown place. Fantastic operation, and one could drown, no doubt, in the shower of nickels and dimes spent there in a half hour. But a bore to the serious player.

• SAHARA. Another of the older hotels on the Strip, but extremely good. Excellent food and games. Jerry Lewis, Buddy Hackett, and Sonny and Cher are among recent performers there.

• SANDS. This was once the best hotel and casino in town, the in-place, with hordes of movie stars vacationing there all the time, and the best shows —Sinatra, Sammy Davis, Jr., Dean Martin, and the like. But then Howard Hughes bought the hotel and it suddenly and mysteriously became dull, attracting mostly small-timers and scattering most of the performing and vacationing stars to other places. A shame, because it was incomparable not too many years ago. The current show stars, for God's sake, Wayne Newton and Dave Barry.

• STARDUST. A big, glittering, frenzied joint on the Strip, but not my cup of tea—and perhaps not yours. Most of the people there seem either to be conventioneers or are attracted to the place by special deals—package tours, bargain-priced rooms and economy meals—and the play is generally small. There's nothing wrong with that, of course, but, for the better player, the atmosphere just isn't conducive to psyching yourself into feeling and operating like a killer at the tables.

• THUNDERBIRD. This is a hotel which has stayed alive on the Strip for a long time, but it's blatantly down-at-the-heels and shabby. You look around, taste the food, or try the tables, and you feel the place should be moved into town.

• TROPICANA. A genuinely beautiful and taste-fully decorated place, but, until recently, so quiet and inactive that you often found yourself playing at tables with shills and employees so downcast that the shills' one-dollar bets didn't even get picked up when they lost. But the hotel is now trying to turn into an action joint with, it's said, Sammy Davis, Jr., given a piece of the place and booked in as the first of a series of big-name entertainers. Not a bad hotel even if all that doesn't materialize, at least for people who like to gamble but enjoy peace and quiet along with the gambling.

• UNION PLAZA. A big, brand-new hotel in town, and lavish, lively, and impressive. But, you know, in town.

Reno, Nevada

Cooler in weather and pace than Las Vegas, but just as legitimate. There are a lot of small, undistinguished places in Reno, but you ought to confine your patronage to the Big Three, all of which are first rate. They are the **Mapes Hotel, Harrah's** and **Harold's Club.** Not too many big-name shows in Reno, and not too many junkets going there, but a pleasant, quiet town for good food and good gambling.

Lake Tahoe, Nevada

This is a miniature Las Vegas, featuring big-time shows and beautiful hotels and casinos. Located in the High Sierra and perfect for people who like to combine boating and fishing (and nearby skiing) with their gaming. The best places here are the **Sahara-Tahoe** and the **King's Castle,** and they're not small. The **Sahara-Tahoe,** for example, has six hundred rooms and advertises that its casino is the largest in Nevada, and I guess it is.

2. ANTIGUA

This small island in the Caribbean is great if you're after sunshine and rest interspersed with a little gambling. But don't go if you want shows, shopping and things like that, because there's little else on the island; employees at the hotels have been known to compare their stay to imprisonment and refer to the place as "The Rock." One other tip. There are a lot of junkets going to Antigua, but go on your own if you go. I've never had any problems personally, but a lot of other people have complained that the casinos are hungry and tend to breathe down the necks of people who are there on the house, even when they're substantial players. The active places there are the **Holiday Inn** and **Maramora Beach Hotel and Casino.**

3. ARGENTINA

There's gambling all over Argentina, but the best casinos are the ones in Mar del Plata, Miramar, and Mendoza.

4. ARUBA

Another very small island in the Caribbean, with not a lot to do, but the beaches are lovely and the gaming is government-supervised and active. The places to visit are the **Holiday Inn** and **Aruba-Caribbean Hotel and Casino.**

5. AUSTRIA

There are casinos in most Austrian resort towns. The casinos in Baden, Bad Gastein, Salzburg, and Velden are particularly good, and so are the casinos in Vienna.

6. THE BAHAMAS

There are a number of big, lavish Las Vegas-type hotels and casinos scattered throughout these Caribbean islands, and most of them are very good. The list includes **Kings Inn** and the **International** in Freeport, the **Paradise Island Hotel and**

Villas and the **Holiday Inn** on Paradise Island, and the **Bahamian Club** in Nassau. There are junkets going regularly to nearly all of these places. My personal preference here is the **International,** where the accommodations and the action seem just a shade better than the other places. But there's one bad thing about the joints in the Bahamas: They take a big extra cut every time you win a bet, as a sort of added fee. And, obviously, it's harder to pile up a bankroll if you pocket less on every win.

7. BELGIUM

Like Austria, there are good casinos in most of the country's resort towns. Try the ones at Chaudfontaine, Knokke, Miederke, Namur, and Oostende.

8. BONAIRE

Still another tiny Caribbean island. The good casino, well supervised by the governing fathers, is at tho **Hotel Bonaire.**

9. BULGARIA

There are passable casinos in most of the resorts on the Black Sea.

10. CAMBODIA

Honestly, do you really intend to go to Cambodia to gamble? The last time I heard, there was an active casino there called, appropriately enough, **Cambodia,** but it may have been destroyed by the cannons of one warring side or the other in that sad country. Also, if you'll forgive me for stating the obvious, please keep in mind that you can get your tushie shot off as you bend over a table.

11. CHILE

Gaming is legal here and there in Chile, but the only really reliable casino, in my opinion, is the one in Vina del Mar.

12. COLOMBIA

A fair number of junkets go to **El Caribe Hotel** in Cartagena, and the casino is large and legitimate. Skip the others.

13. CURAÇAO

Curaçao, the little Dutch island in the Caribbean, is only thirty-eight miles long, but it's a picturesque spot with a lot of pretty beaches and plenty of gaming. There are junkets going there every week of the year, and the best places are the **Curaçao-Hilton,** the **Flamboyant Sands,** and the **Intercontinental.**

14. DOMINICAN REPUBLIC

This Caribbean island is tightly held by a dictatorship, which makes a lot of people nervous, including me. If you don't react that way, there's plenty of sunshine, swimming and gambling, and the best action is in the casinos at **Hotel Embajador, Hotel Hispaniola, Hotel Europa, Aqua Loz Night Club,** and **Voz Dominica Night Club.**

15. ECUADOR

There are two good casinos in Ecuador. One is in Guayaquil and is open the year round, and the other is in Playas and is open from May to December each year.

16. EGYPT

There are plenty of casinos in Cairo, Alexandria, and some of the smaller Egyptian cities. But watch your wallet.

17. FRANCE

There are nearly two hundred casinos throughout France, but, as stated earlier, they don't dig dice. So if you're vacationing or on business on the Riviera, you've got to do as I do: Rent a car or hire a car and chauffeur and make the fifteen- or twenty-mile trek to Monte Carlo, about which more later. And if you're in Paris, concentrate on the food or the beautiful girls. Or both.

18. GERMANY

There's plenty of gambling in Germany for your **Frau** or **Fräulein** and yourself. You'll find a large casino in virtually every resort town in the country as well as in a lot of the other towns. Some of the best are located in Baden-Baden, Bad Homburg, Hannover, Lindau, and Wiesbaden.

19. GHANA

Yes, people **do** go to Ghana to gamble. I know of at least one man who went once, and the place he recommends is **Casino Africa** in Accra.

20. GREAT BRITAIN

There are well over three hundred casinos in Great Britain, many with Americans on the staff, stressing dice as a main staple in their operation. Most of the best ones are in London. Up to a couple of years ago there were junkets going to London all the time, but the government, with its unerring instinct for losing business and income, put a stop to this by passing a law requiring foreign visitors to be in the country for forty-eight hours before being allowed to enter gambling establishments. (Don't ask me the reason for the law. I suppose it's to prevent foreigners from entering the land solely for the shocking purpose of gambling. But whatever the reason, it's strictly enforced, with inspectors hovering about and casino operators losing their licenses if they let a stray foreigner pop in his first day in the country.) Anyway, the result of the restriction was to put an end to junkets, since the restriction meant that junket operators would have to house and feed junketeers for two full days (nearly half the length of a typical junket period) without getting a return crack at them during that time, and that made things unprofitable. It's still worthwhile going on your own, of course, since London is one of the most delightful cities in the world, with great theatre, restaurants and sightseeing—in short, great everything, including the action. Some of the best places are the **Colony Club, Crockford's, Curzon House, International Sporting Club, Les Ambassadeurs, Olympic Casino, A Pair of Shoes, Palm Beach Casino Club,** the **Playboy Club, 21 Club,** and **Victoria Sporting**

Club—all in London. There's also a very good place, which used to be called **Las Vegas of Great Britain** and is now called **Palace Hotel and Casino**, on the Isle of Man. You'll need a membership card to enter most establishments, but the hall porter at most hotels will get this for you in a couple of minutes (the cost is usually about a pound).

21. GREECE

Lots of gambling here. The best places are **Mont Parnes Casino** in Athens, **Achilleon Palace in** Corfu, and the **Grand Hotel Summer Palace** in Rhodes. My favorite is **Mont Parnes;** the only trouble with it, as the name suggests, is that it's on top of a mountain and can only be reached by a hair-raising ride on a cable car or an equally horrifying drive on a road that seems straight up and interminable. You'd better go somewhere else if you tend to get sweaty palms when you're confronted by heights.

22. HAITI

I really don't think you'll want to go to Haiti, where the hunger and the poverty is so horrifying all around you that you won't have much heart for fun and games. If you do go, the only place is the **Casino International** in Port-au-Prince. But don't go.

23. ITALY

There are casinos at many Italian resorts, among
them St. Vincent, San Remo, and Taorima. Most
people like Italy so much that it's almost fun losing there. Almost, but not quite.

24. LEBANON

Lebanon is loaded with gambling houses, but the
only reliable place in the country is the **Casino du
Liban,** just outside of Beirut.

25. MACAO

Macao is one of the most active gambling centers
in the world, exactly as portrayed in all those old
movies starring people like Brian Donlevy, Lyle
Talbot, and Dick Purcell. I think there are eleven
million gambling joints in Macao—an exaggeration, of course, but only a small exaggeration.
Watch your wallet here, too.

26. MONACO

Monaco is, of course, the tiny principality (less
than 3/5ths of a square mile in area) which con-
tains the famous **Monte Carlo Casino.** But if the

words "Monte Carlo" conjure up a glamourous picture in your mind, you're going to be enormously disappointed when you visit the place itself. The truth of the matter is that the **Monte Carlo Casino** may indeed have been a place of glamour back in the Teens and Twenties, when all the books were written about it and all the movies made about it. But today, judged by modern standards of architecture and modern interior decoration, the place is just sadly seedy. The marble and tile interior is yellowing and not too clean, reminding some stunned observers of nothing so much as the men's room in an old-fashioned movie palace; the place is loaded with hookers, sometimes doing their soliciting right in the gambling rooms; and players who aren't being bothered by ladies of the night are harassed by near-panhandlers who rush forward to give unnecessary help—like straightening one's pile of chips—in the hope that a chip will be thrown to them. And for dice players the place is a particular disappointment. The game has obviously been included (grudgingly) only because a certain number of Americans visit the casino, so the dice tables are open for only a short time daily and the play is small and lackadaisical. The verdict, I guess, is apparent. If you're in France, and absolutely aching for a shot at the cubes, go over to Monaco and make the best of the mediocre fare served up to you at the **Monte Carlo Casino.** Otherwise, give your attention to the place only when there's a dated movie about it on the Late Late Show and you're suffering from insomnia and can't fall asleep.

27. MOROCCO

Loaded with gambling houses, the best of which are **Casino of Mohammadia,** located on the outskirts of Casablanca, **Casino Tangier** in Tangier, and **Casino Marrakech** in (how'd you ever guess?) Marrakech. But if you haven't had your wallet swiped in Egypt or Macao, you'll certainly lose it here.

28. NIGERIA

There's gambling all over the place, but none of it is supervised by officials of any kind. Only a nut would risk his money under these conditions.

29. PANAMA

Once considered pretty remote territory, but more and more junkets are starting to go there now. The most popular joint in the country is the **El Panama** (formerly the **El Panama Hilton)** in Panama City. It's kept its popularity despite the fact that the management had to move the casino from the top floor of the building to the ground floor after a loser settled his account by jumping to his death. Other popular casinos include the **Continental,** the **Siesta,** and the **Granada.**

30. THE PHILIPPINES

There are casinos all over Manila. Caution is advised at every one of them. To tell the truth, what's really advised is non-attendance.

31. PORTUGAL

The casino in Estoril is a popular place the year round, with visitors from all over the world; a number of junkets take you there. Other good casinos in Portugal are in Figueira da Foz, Povoa do Varzim, and Espinho, but they're open only during the summers.

32. PUERTO RICO

Puerto Rico is, of course, full of big, beautiful hotels, most of which have big, busy casinos. The most popular places are **El San Juan**, the **Americana**, the **Sheraton**, the **Isla Helio San Jeronimo**, and the **Caribe Hilton**, all in San Juan; the **Dorado del Mar** (formerly the **Dorado Hilton**) and the **Dorado Beach Hotel** in Dorado Beach; and **El Conquistador** in Las Croabas. My personal favorites are **El San Juan** and **El Conquistador**, both with the same management. I've heard—though I haven't had this problem personally—that they're the type of outfit described earlier: shifters with the wind. If, in other words, you're a gambling guest and their last few weeks have been profitable, they'll wear out your door delivering fruits, booze and flowers, but, I'm told, you can't get them on the phone when times have been temporarily tough. Junkets run to most of the hotels.

One big problem about Puerto Rico: The game they play there is one they call "simplified," but which is actually changed to eliminate some of the good things you get in places like Las Vegas and London. To give just two examples among many: they pay even money on six and eight **place** bets, making them nothing more than another **Big 6 And Big 8** with those unpleasantly high percentages against you, and there's no such thing as buying numbers. Most people leave cold climes and go to Puerto Rico in the winter months, and you've got to decide for yourself if sun and warmth in wintertime make up for these disadvantages.

33. ST. MAARTEN

Another small Caribbean island to which junkets go week after week. The **St. Maarten Isle** and the **Concord Hotel** are the best places here.

34. SURINAM

This is one more Caribbean island. The place to play here is the **Torarica Hotel** in Paramirabo. An okay place: passable if you happen to be in Surinam doing whatever people do in Surinam, but not worth a special trip.

35. SWITZERLAND

There are a number of casinos in Switzerland. They're not, however, for those exclusively into dice because the only game permitted in the casinos is boule, a pastime so obscure that I've just looked in three dictionaries, for the hell of it, and find the word listed in none of them. (For those who care, though I don't know why you should, boule is a variation of roulette in which a ball spins around and falls into one of eighteen slots. Hooray.)

36. SYRIA

There's plenty of gambling in Syria, which is all I care to say about Syria.

37. TURKEY

I might as well admit it: Istanbul scares the hell out of me, though I don't really know why. I guess it's because it's such a dark, ominous place that I expect to get my throat cut every time I turn into a shadowy street—and Istanbul is full of shadowy streets. I confess to all this even though I've never been accosted by anyone in Istanbul, not even by a lady whose profession is accosting. There are a number of large casinos such as the one at the **Istanbul Hilton,** but you can have my place at the tables there.

38. URUGUAY

There's gambling all over Uruguay, but the best and most reliable action is at two spots in Montevideo: the **Park Hotel** and the **Carrasco Hotel.**

39. YUGOSLAVIA

Despite its ominous name, the best joint in Yugoslavia is the **Casino Bled** in Dubrovnik. (Oddly enough, the people I know who went there didn't get bled at all. They won substantially.) Another good casino is in Krk, a town which you have to click rather than pronounce: the **Palace Hotel and Casino** (formerly called the **Penthouse Club,** and previously owned and operated by **Penthouse Magazine**). Other good casinos in Yugoslavia are the **Hotel Adriatic Casino** in Umago and **Brioni Hotel and Casino** in Pula.

Just for the record, the following is a list of some of the places which, I'm told, don't have legalized gambling: Afghanistan, Barbados, Bolivia, British Guiana, British Windward Islands, Burma, Canada, the Congo, Costa Rica, Denmark, El Salvador, Ethiopia, Fiji Islands, Finland, French Guiana, Guadeloupe, Guatemala, Guiana, Hong Kong, Hungary, India, Indonesia, Ireland, Kenya, Liberia, Libya, Luxembourg, Martinique, Mexico, Nepal, Netherlands, New Zealand, Nicaragua, Norway, Paraguay, Peru, Samoa, Senegal, South Africa, Spain, Sri Lanka, Sweden, Tahiti, Taiwan, Thailand, Tobago, Trinidad, USSR, Venezuela, and the Virgin Islands. Silly fellows.

INDEX